ETIOLOGY

ETIOLOGY

TRACKING A DEADLY PATHOGEN

EVAN NAVORI

NEW DEGREE PRESS

COPYRIGHT © 2020 EVAN NAVORI

ETIOLOGY

Tracking a Deadly Pathogen

ISBN 978-1-63676-551-8 *Paperback*

     978-1-63676-122-0 *Kindle Ebook*

     978-1-63676-123-7 *Ebook*

To my mom and dad, thank you for everything.

CONTENTS

e·ti·ol·o·gy (noun): the cause of a
disease or medical condition.

CHAPTER 1:

BEGINNINGS

———

Inaudible chatter plays on the loudspeaker above: "Can . . . please come . . . help desk." At the moment, I'm so dazed and irritated I couldn't even hear what the person said.

You see, I'm about to board a sixteen-hour flight entirely sober, which is not a fun experience, if you ask me. However, we all do stupid things when we're young.

Oh, I should probably explain why I'm here at the Los Angeles International Airport and complaining about being locked in a giant, steel tube for the next sixteen hours.

You see, I am a graduate of the University of Michigan's Medical School, a true doctor of medicine. I graduated a couple of years ago and did my thing for several years working in hospitals around the country. However, I got bored, so I decided to apply for a research position at the University of Queensland in Brisbane, Australia, back in February. Now, I did this partly because it's sunny there. Having spent the last couple of years locked in the oasis that is Ann Arbor, Michigan, I needed a break. However, the main reason why I applied for this position was because they were looking for someone with a special set of skills: an infectious disease doctor (i.e. me).

Now, this may not be the most glamorous position out there, working with things that will most likely end the world, but it pays the bills. Plus, it'll be a nice hiatus away from the hustle and bustle of my hometown—Nashville, Tennessee.

Right now, I'm at the gate (gate thirty-five, to be exact) and I've commandeered an entire section of chairs near the large windows. I'm not one for sharing, nor am I the most social of people. As I sit down in the unconformable metal and faux leather chairs, staring out into the black abyss of a Los Angeles night sky, I reminisce on the fact that I managed to make it on time. My college professors would be so proud of me.

The scenery from my uncomfortable chair is nothing too spectacular. Almost everything—the shops, signs, and most of the chairs—is covered in a satin white tarp in order to prevent dust particles from the construction interfering with LAX's intrepid travelers. However, the construction hasn't stopped people from flying: it is bustling.

My flight is supposed to board in fifteen minutes, but I'm at LAX, which is notorious for its delays. Who knows what will happen? Definitely not me. All I know is it's 10:45 p.m. on August 21, 2019, and I am frazzled. The dark, gray bags under my eyes are, unfortunately, not designer, and the red, bloodshot tinge around my pupils only makes things worse. It's been a long day: I woke up at 5:00 a.m. to the sound of an obnoxious mockingbird outside my bedroom window, and I almost missed my ride to the airport because of a seldom-studied phenomenon known as "last-minute packing."

Here's another story while I patiently wait for my flight to board: Earlier today, as I was eating my not-so-healthy lunch, I read up on some scientific literature. Well, while I was perusing the latest propaganda from my favorite magazine,

National Geographic, I saw something intriguing: no, it wasn't *entirely* about penguins; it was actually about how my field, medicine, will be fundamentally altered because of climate change. Now, upon further reading its enigmatic title (something about mosquitoes or mammoths. . . . I don't remember), I perked up and immediately clicked on the article. Sigh. It turns out it was all speculative, and there is no concrete evidence between climate change and medicine, yet. However, it was quite interesting how they mentioned . . .

"Qantas flight sixteen with a scheduled service to Brisbane, Australia, is now boarding." Booyah.

I guess I'll have to finish that story later as well.

Accoutering myself with my blue sport coat and brown leather messenger bag, I begin the arduous journey of standing in a queue. Fortunately for me, the line moves pretty fast.

As I walk up to the gate agent with my ticket in hand, I realize that I did not download any movies or TV shows for the flight. To put the cherry on top, I even forgot to bring headphones. Not only does this mean I can't drown out the incessant drone of the two big General Electric engines, but it also means that I can't listen to my favorite artist, the infamous Kanye West.

When I reach the front of the line, I hand my ticket to the fairly young gate agent, who kindly replies, "Thank you for flying with Qantas, Doctor . . . um." Ouch. That was a nice gesture considering my last name looks like an amalgamation of every letter in the English language. Back in college, you should have seen the look on my professors' faces when they had to say, "Is Mr. . . . Kaczanowski . . . here?" Because of the lack of phonetics on literally everything (don't even get me started on this), I decided to go by Dr. Lawrence, Lawrence being my first name.

As I meander down the slightly dank, metal jetway, I see my ride, the engineering feat that is the Boeing 787 Dreamliner, dressed in a white livery with a lone kangaroo on the cherry red tail. You know, I've never been on one before, so this should be mildly entertaining. However, my excitement soon fades, and I want nothing more than to sleep for the next sixteen hours.

An even longer queue, reminiscent of Friday afternoon traffic, slowly starts to develop in the cramped jetway, causing me to rethink everything. With nothing better to do, I finally glance at my ticket, which was graciously donated by the folks at the University of Queensland. I'm not in first class, apparently. Shame. Instead, my humble abode for the next sixteen hours is 47A, presumably out in BFE.

At least, to my knowledge, it should be a window seat, which means that I get a free view and one fewer person to talk to. Nice.

When I finally settle into the narrow window seat, my body starts to decompress and relax, conforming to the seat's rigid shape. I continue breathing in and out, slipping into "Zen mode," until my seatmate, a gregarious looking man named Thomas, finally arrives. Thomas is an older gentleman, perhaps a septuagenarian. He's wearing a red golf polo and a pair of khaki pants. A bit ostentatious for a flight or even a round of golf. Maybe. However, that's not the problem. Thomas, he is a chatter box . . . just what I wished for. Usually, I truly am quite fond of the occasional chin-wag when it is warranted; however, it's almost midnight, and I need my beauty sleep.

My loquacious seatmate starts peppering me with all sorts of awkward questions while we taxi out to the runway. I don't know about you, but I don't want to answer strange and unusual questions on an airplane. I just want to sleep. So, I do what any adult would do, I tell the man that I'm tired and have had a rough day.

Sure enough, he stops. It looks like chivalry isn't dead.

Unfortunately, my brief bit of respite lasts for a mere five hours. Now, I am not a mathematician, but I am pretty sure that means I still have eleven hours to go.

To make things better, my seatmate, noticing that I am now awake, decides to relaunch his initial interrogation campaign. To counteract his barrage of unwarranted and unsolicited questions, I deftly pull out my computer from my leather messenger bag in order to look busy.

For the record, I haven't cleaned my MacBook's desktop in years. The desktop is replete with files that are strewn haphazardly in every direction. It kind of looks like my organic chemistry binder after the first lecture.

After I spend some time randomly clicking some files to look "busy," I find something interesting: my old research notes from biology.

I know it may not be the latest and greatest *Star Wars* movie, but it's all I've got right now. Also, I don't see the stewardesses sashaying around with free headphones, so this is what the next eleven hours will have to consist of.

I immediately click the folder titled "Lab Notes," because I remember taking detailed photos of almost every experiment I did. I reason that at least looking at photos will keep me preoccupied for long enough.

Well, sure enough, I have a photographical repository of some pretty cool things from my cellular dynamics research. You think *The Hunger Games* is exhilarating? Well, wait until you see a *bursaria truncatella* (a large, single-celled organism that looks like a blob of goop) devour a *paramecium* (another small, single-celled organism that looks like a grain of rice). The size difference is discernible: you can clearly see the *bursaria's* stomach abounding with several previously digested *paramecia.* To provide a more scientific description on the *bursaria,* I'll say that it is festooned with tiny hairlike structures called cilia, which allow us to eat and move. The *bursaria* effortlessly locomotes (or swims, as it's called in the scientific community) like a graceful shark hunting on a tuna. Blobs and rice. Science is beautiful. I'm a thirty-three-year-old man getting excited about a three-minute video of microorganisms moving. Lovely.

However, the *bursaria truncatella,* let's call him Teddy, can't satiate my curiosity. Teddy is only a jovial and briefly entertaining creature, no more. I need something time consuming yet intriguing. Like the great archeologist Indiana Jones, I painstakingly look through each file, looking for anything else that could amuse me.

Well, after much tribulation, I find what I'm looking for: a mere portion of my genome. Now, you may be asking yourself, "Why does this man have access to his own genome, and why does he want to sit there and read it?"

The answer to the first question is quite simple: I sent my DNA a while back to a new biotech startup that traces your ancestry and DNA and I wanted to check some of their work; not all of it, of course. I'm not that much of a perfectionist. The answer to the second question is even less complicated. Like I said earlier, I still have eleven hours to go, and I can only sleep for so long.

* * *

My screen is currently filled with nitrogenous bases: thousands of A's, T's, G's, and C's forming a neat row, all abreast. Technically, a human genome consists of billions of them, but I'm only looking at a smidge, so . . . While I sit here sifting through the entire genome, my eager seatmate appears perplexed and even more inquisitive.

"Excuse me sir, um, what do all those letters mean?" he says as he adjusts his thick bifocal glasses.

"This is a DNA sequence," I quickly reply.

His head cocks to the side, the wrinkles around his eyes become more pronounced, and his eyebrows raise in an apparent state of confusion. It is almost like I told him that bigfoot was actually a government conspiracy. He is clearly mystified.

"Oh, but what *is* it?"

"DNA? It is an acronym that stands for deoxyribonucleic acid. Sounds pretty neat, I know. It basically stores information, sort of like a line of code on a computer."

"Oh," he says as he shakes his head. "But wait. What type of information does it store then?"

"Well, DNA stores hereditary information. It's kind of like a genetic blueprint that stores the instructions for almost everything in a cell. And it stores all of this information in a genetic vault called the nucleus. Now, DNA's information is stored in a way that's similar to binary code. It's not stored in ones and zeros, sadly. That would have made it too easy, and I wouldn't be payed the big bucks to decipher it. Rather, it's in the form of nitrogenous bases, including but not limited to adenine—A—thymine—T—guanine—G—and cytosine—C. Adenine always binds to thymine, and guanine always binds to cytosine. A great little pneumonic to remember it: apple in the tree, car in the garage."[1]

"Here," I say, "look at this picture of DNA. It's even color coded."

Thomas, the stocky septuagenarian, leans in closer, squinting his blue eyes.

Out of nowhere, he says, "It looks like the box pasta. The fusilli kind."

I immediately sit up in my chair and a smirk starts to appear on my face. Fusilli. Never heard that one before.

"That describes it, but I prefer my analogy: DNA is kind of like a spiral staircase. The nitrogenous bases, which we previously talked about, are the steps, and the sugar-phosphate backbone is the railing. This spiral staircase goes on for billions and billions of base pairs, forming the classic double helix.

"Now, DNA isn't just hanging around like little threads of dental floss. A single DNA strand is actually wrapped around proteins, called histones, but that doesn't matter. Anyway, this ungodly creation forms a nucleosome, and after many of twists and turns, this nucleosome forms a chromosome."[2]

Thomas starts nodding his head up and down in agreement. "You should become a teacher," he says as he points his wrinkled finger at me.

With a half-hearted smile, I reply, "Ah, I thought about that a long time ago. Never really followed through on it."

---

1   "Deoxyribonucleic Acid (DNA) Fact Sheet," National Human Genome Research Institute, Date Last Modified August 24, 2020.

2   "Histone," National Human Genome Research Institute, Date Accessed September 22, 2020.

He then purses his lips, taking on a vow of silence as he shifts his gaze back toward the seat in front of him.

My unwarranted lecture turns my seatmate silent. I guess my famous quote reigns supreme:

Science turns even extroverts into introverts.

Upon gazing at my knockoff silver Rolex, I am reminded that I still have nine hours left. Great.

With no movies, music, or microorganisms to watch, I do what any rational person would do. I sleep again.

Boy, do I sleep. I guess crossing the International Date Line must have taken its toll on my circadian rhythms—a topic for another day. Apparently, my internal clock must have reset, because I slept for nearly eight hours, which means that my flight is scheduled to land very, very soon.

All I have to do now is just look out the window and admire the deep blue waters of the Pacific Ocean for the next hour—a piece of cake, if you ask me.

* * *

The plane finally lands in Brisbane at 5:30 a.m., local time. It's too early for most people and, apparently, even the sun. A dark, gloomy gaze still engulfs the sky as it transitions from night to day. Although the stars have receded into the night sky, the airport's floodlights fill their role and light up the surrounding area.

When we finally pull into the gate, I pack up the rest of my things and manage to waddle down the jetway at a snail's pace. Still very much dazed, I dexterously grab what appears to be my bag from the conveyor belt: a black suitcase with a creamsicle-colored tag.

* * *

Outside of the airport is a different atmosphere than the calm and tranquil interior. One by one, the plane's passengers file through the sliding glass doors, creating a chaotic environment.

As I walk out of the airport, I engage in a fun game of human bumper cars as other passengers constantly bounce off other people. Not the greatest experience if you're a germaphobe.

The sun slowly begins to crawl its way through the dense atmosphere. Although the sun's rays begin to illuminate the exterior, I don't see anyone with a sign that says, "Dr. Lawrence."

I'm not disappointed. Sure, I've been stood up before. In fact, I was actually stood up by . . .

"Dr. Lawrence!" echoes out in the distance.

I immediately take on the posture of a scarred meerkat, scanning the horizon.

There he is: Dr. Lancaster. A man in his late fifties with a slick comb-over and a slightly lean figure. He looks very disheveled with his unkempt light gray tie and the top button of his baby blue shirt undone. It is almost like something important is eating at the poor fellow from the inside. What is bothering him? Was he nervous to meet this dashing young doctor? Possibly, but not likely.

As I walk up to him, I attempt to shake the man's hand, yet he rejects my proposed handshake. He doesn't even tell me why.

I guess my new boss is a germaphobe. Sigh.

"So, you're the new guy, huh? I should've expected more," he says as his eyes scan up and down my body.

Now, I'm not entirely sure what he means by that, but I don't think it was a compliment. I can already tell that these next couple of months are going to be rough.

He kindly offers to take my luggage to his car. What a sweetheart. To my surprise, his car, unlike himself, is absolutely spotless. It's an older, jet-black Land Rover Defender. The car may be older than me, but her engine purrs like a year-old kitten.

We pull out of the three-story parking garage and merge onto the main highway, heading toward town. At six in the morning, not a single soul is on the road. Unfortunately, Dr. Lancaster turned down my request to "floor it." However, the scenery is beautiful. A thick line of trees station themselves on the right side of the road, creating an ominous and eerie parallel: human encroachment on a once pristine land. To the left is the Brisbane River, a sprawling and meandering water feature that connects Brisbane to the coast. Although Dr. Lancaster says that crocodiles don't travel this far south, I still won't be dipping into a river with a Hudson-esque tinge to it. The brown, murky look does not invoke my inner Michael Phelps. I am, however, finally seeing the sun for the first time in several years. The sun continues its ascent into the sky, creating a peach- and pink-colored hue. With a warm and fuzzy feeling developing inside of me, I realize I'm finally enjoying my life, even with the constant movement from place to place.

Although the scenery is picturesque, the conversation is dreadful. Dr. Lancaster is a stereotypical introvert. Talking to him is like talking to a bush—not very pleasant, and every response is one word, nothing more. The conversation goes something like this: "Wow, this town is incredible. What type of trees are those? The ones with the light grey and tan bark?" I ask. Dr. Lawrence replies, "No clue."

The good news, however, is that it's a short ride into the sprawling central business district with skyscrapers flanking the left side of the river.

* * *

Just as I'm getting comfortable in Dr. Lancaster's archaic Land Rover, he tells me we're almost there. Sure enough, the car eventually pulls into an open parking spot on a side street.

"We're here, Dr. Lawrence," Dr. Lancaster says, rather sternly.

Upon exiting the rugged SUV, I immediately retrieve my luggage, and then I see it. My home for the next four months: the Australian Infectious Diseases Research Centre (AID).

When I first imagined the building a couple of months ago, I thought it would've been a shabby, old, concrete building. You know, something out of Area 51. Boy, am I wrong. And I'm never wrong.

Granted, it's not the Ritz-Carlton, but it'll get the job done. The building is ultramodern with a slick glass exterior and metal accents. She's completely spotless; the University of Queensland apparently refitted the lab back in 2011, making sure to include the latest state-of-the-art technology, from negative pressure systems to the finest PCR machines. More on the particulars later, but for now, you get the gist. Everything is glass and steel. It kind of looks like something out of *Architectural Digest*, a must-read if you haven't already.

"Follow me," says Dr. Lancaster.

Dr. Lancaster escorts me past the guard desk and through security. Any place that has a guard desk and requires a security clearance means business. I wonder, Are they trying to prevent people from coming in or leaving? Hmm . . .

As I walk down the halls of the AID, I notice something: it's completely barren. The walls are bleached white, and there are no pictures or anything. The only sound is the incessant drone of the LED lights in the distance. It feels institutional.

The halls form a unique labyrinth, sort of like a festive corn maze during the winter months. Although I'm pretty sure Dr. Lancaster is lost right now. I would ask to help him, but I don't want to abase him. Also, I get paid by the hour here, so I'm fine with anything.

I do, however, finally see my first dash of color: purple, and lots of it. It is the AID's mission statement plastered across the wall in a grandiose manner. A bit much? Maybe, but I'll let you decide.

In big, bold, purple letters it says: "Utilise leading technologies to identify, understand, and prevent infectious disease," or something like that.

Dr. Lancaster turns right at the propaganda intersection and heads to the end of the hall. I, of course, have to follow him. I can tell, though, that he doesn't trust me yet.

We enter into an unmarked room at the end of the hallway. The room is cozy yet not claustrophobic. The walls are painted the same white color, and there's a circular, wooden table in the middle, flanked by four chairs. He sits me down in the ostensible waiting room. At first glance, it seems pretty innocuous.

Then, he says, "We don't want you wandering off."

I guess I look like the type of person who is mischievous. Good to know.

He does also mention that some of the staff are finalizing my documents, such as my ID badge, which I haven't even received yet.

For several minutes, we just sit there and stare blankly at each other, sizing the other person up.

Then, another man, whose name I did not catch, drops off the last of my paperwork in a manilla folder. The boorish-looking man with a scruffy beard doesn't stay for long and quickly absconds, leaving Dr. Lancaster and me in a precarious situation. After wading through the deep pile of paperwork, Dr. Lancaster suddenly turns conversational, like an inquisitive FBI agent interrogating a suspect. Do I really need to explain myself to the man who read through my entire application?

I'm a good sport, though, so I play along.

He asks me if I had any real laboratory experience, because my answers on the application were a bit vague. You see, I don't really know how to respond, since I don't really have any. I have clinical experience instead, with a smidge of lab experience from my college days, so I decide to give him one of my canned responses.

"I volunteered in West Africa in 2014 to combat the Ebola epidemic. I was boots on the ground—collecting blood samples and running diagnostic and antibody tests. I've also done some work in South America, focused on other hemorrhagic fevers and the like."

"But you have no real lab experience, right?" Dr. Lancaster says.

"Yes, that's true. I'm an MD with clinical experience. If you need me to diagnose a patient or take blood samples and analyze them, I'm your guy. If need be, I do have some laboratory experience from my undergrad years, but that was yonks ago."

His ears perk up.

Finally, I got to him. I cracked the nut that is Dr. Lancaster.

That's when he lays it on me.

"Look, kid, we do a lot of important lab work here, emphasis on *lab* work. We change lives here, and this morning, we just received some highly confidential and time-sensitive information that will require an extensive amount of field work. We're all pretty focused on that right now. Given your extensive background in the field, I think you'll make a great fit. However, there are some staunch opponents of you being in the lab, so you'll have to prove you're not a liability."

He then asks, "What did you say your specialty was again?"

I nervously reply, "Emerging infectious diseases, emphasis on emerging."

Without any hesitation, he says, "Perfect. Be in the meeting room in ten minutes."

Like a true professional, he immediately flees, leaving me with more questions than answers.

Then I realize that he never told me where the meeting room was.

* * *

Here I am, a man on a mission. A mission to not be late, for once.

Now, I'm pretty sure I saw a map of the floor somewhere in the hallway. So, like the great explorer Amerigo Vespucci, I set off on a journey to find the meeting location.

I traverse the halls, moving from room to room, yet I find nothing.

Minutes pass, and I must admit that I am not the seasoned explorer that I think I am. I am currently lost. Tracing your steps is hard when you're in a building where every room is painted with the same monotone color—eggshell, or something like that.

In the midst of searching, something usurps my attention: hunger. They don't feed you much on those long-haul flights, and I'm a growing man.

Now, my mission has changed slightly, but the goals remain the same: make it on time and find food. Simple.

After searching for some time, I finally find a near-empty room that looks promising. Like any inquisitive houseguest, I immediately let myself in and start tinkering with some of the neat pens and files on a crowded desk.

I'm not quite sure what this room is used for. There's no scientific equipment or anything of that nature, so it's not a lab. Everything also seems drab and dull. There are no family pictures next to the computer, and there's no pictures on the wall. If you ask me, it needs some HGTV love, but I'm not here to judge.

As I regard the bleakness of the room, I find something quite interesting. No, much to my dismay, this room isn't the meeting room. What I do find is the forbidden fruit: an abandoned banana. It is, of course, a standard-issue, imported banana. It's nothing fancy, but it is enough to satiate my appetite.

As I sit here eating the rescued banana, I, once again, become sidetracked. A sixteen-hour flight and lack of nutrition has a deleterious effect on your mental abilities. The mere idea of the meeting slips my mind as I start reading some of the papers that were laid across the desk in a disorganized manner. One of the papers is, however, quite interesting. It's about the Mendelian genetics of mangos. Kind of strange if you ask me, but when you're dealing with the notorious flying foxes, or fruit bats, of Queensland, it provides a clue to their location.

After I continue to sift through the papers, I finally realize what this room's purpose is. It's an office. Not mine, yet. It actually belongs to Dr. Rebecca Fraser, whoever that is.

My starvation continues to dictate my actions, and I begin to act in an aberrant manner: I start spinning around in the chair like a grown child. However, someone interrupts my ostensible playtime. Dr. Fraser strolls past the door and catches me in the act. She immediately backtracks and stands there with her hands on her hips, judging me with her green eyes. Although I was just caught reading someone else's documents while eating their banana, I have been in worse situations.

My mind immediately draws a blank, and I begin jumbling my words, managing to only produce a "how's it going?"

Dr. Rebecca Fraser stands there, arms akimbo, wearing a white lab coat.

Dr. Fraser says, "What are you, uh, doing with my banana?"

"I'm an auditor who is tasked with verifying his scientific research about the Hendra virus," I reply.

"Cool beans, but why are you eating my banana?"

"Ghrelin? The hunger-inducing hormone."

"Sure, that's a scientific answer, but it doesn't answer the root of my question," she says, sternly.

"That's all I got. I'm the new guy from the United States."

"Oh, you're the Yank," she says as she begins to rub her face with her right hand. "Well, I guess my potassium deficiency will have to get filled some other way," she says.

She starts walking away and yells, "Come on, new guy!"

See, I am a decent explorer.

The meeting room is pretty standard, nothing too fancy. I kind of expected more, considering the exterior of the building, but I'm not here to judge.

Like before, there is a singular round table centered in the middle. The only discernible difference is the number of chairs—five. Only five chairs mean that I only need to learn the names of four new people.

Dr. Fraser files into the room first, followed by me.

After much deliberation, I decide to sit next to my new friend, Dr. Fraser.

Upon sitting down in the wobbly chair, Dr. Fraser says, "New guy, you owe me a new banana. That was my snack for today."

"Well, if anything, I deserve a reward," I reply.

She tilts her head and appears dumbfounded.

"You know, I rescued the banana. It was technically abandoned by its owner. Plants have feelings too," I add.

"That's not how it works. I was saving it for later, and now you owe me a new one," she replies.

"I'll think about it. I'm not made of gold bars, and I definitely . . ."

One by one, the other two researchers come in. I think they're the dynamic duo who works with known infectious diseases, like malaria and whatnot. Like all scientists in this building, they are apparently introverts who don't like talking to the new guy. Who knew?

Eventually, the star of the show arrives, Dr. Lancaster. Sporting his white lab coat and khakis, he grabs the only available seat, which is next to me.

A great silence engulfs the room as Dr. Lancaster empties the contents of a manilla folder in front of us. It is almost as if everyone is on the same page except for me. It's sort of like I haven't even opened the book yet. You've been there, right?

He starts the meeting off with some candid introductions.

"Alright, as you may know, we have a new member of the team joining us. This is Dr. Lawrence, who hails from the United States, a true Yank. He's going to be our new field guy. . . ." says Dr. Lancaster.

I'll skip most of the pleasantries, but you get the idea. It's a very cold and calculated introduction from the big man.

However, the tone starts to change when he begins to discuss the week's agenda.

"Alright, now that the pointless introductions are over, let's move on. Yesterday, I got a call from the head of the Russian Centres for Disease Control and Prevention. He said that the agency is currently tracking a new pathogen that emerged in a remote part of Siberia. Now, at the moment, they don't know whether it's viral, bacterial, fungal, or whatever. All they know is that it kills . . ."

"Do they need our help?" Dr. Williams, a member of the dynamic duo, asks.

"That's where it gets interesting. The answer will probably be yes, but they haven't given us permission to send a team in," Dr. Lancaster says.

"Do we know what happened yet?" Dr. Fraser asks.

"No, we don't know anything. Like I said earlier, they know nothing about its genetic makeup. We don't even know if we are going to get a sample of it," he says.

"How long has it been since the original index case was reported?" I ask.

"We don't know. That's why I called this meeting," Dr. Lancaster says.

"This issue primarily concerns our emerging infectious disease department. That's you, Dr. Fraser, and now Dr. Lawrence . . ."

Dr. Fraser lets out an audible sigh as she gives me a half-hearted smile.

"In case the Russian government requests our help, which we would expect given the potential severity of it, we need you two to be on standby. I have already talked with the PM, and we have expedited your travel visas as a precautionary measure."

"Wait, I just got here. Does this mean I'm going to Siberia?" I ask.

"I'm afraid so, Dr. Lawrence. We don't know how dangerous this thing is, so the PM has asked for boots on the ground as soon as we get the clearance," Dr. Lancaster says.

The tables have turned as I let out an audible sigh, and Dr. Fraser smirks.

"Pack your bags. You two leave in a week. That's all," says Dr. Lancaster as he quickly exits the meeting room.

Did you hear that? Just when I think that I finally get some sun, I get sent off to Siberia.

CHAPTER 2

A PREDICAMENT

After Dr. Lancaster's meeting, the AID crew, including me, packs up its belongings and heads home for the weekend.

One by one, we file out of the meeting room like salmon swimming up a salmon ladder— another environmental phenomenon worth witnessing.

Without the aid of any cartograph, I peregrinate through the familiar halls on my way to the exit. Passing the same cream-colored walls, I manage to suppress any thoughts about what just happened.

Not until I pass through security on my way out of the building does it dawn on me: Did I grab the right suitcase?

When I arrived earlier this morning, I grabbed a standard size black suitcase with what appeared to be a creamsicle-colored tag. However, upon further examination under the bright Australian summer sun, I realized that my name is indeed not Chester Wellington, and I did not leave from Bali, Indonesia. Something most definitely went awry.

To make matters worse, my personal chauffeur, Dr. Lancaster, is nowhere to be found, which leaves me standing on the freshly tarred road. With no taxi in sight, I wander the streets looking for any sign of hope. The lush greenery surrounding the AID facility eventually turns into concrete jungle, with massive glass and modern buildings edging either side of the road and a large suspension-like bridge in the distance. The tall buildings block every ray of the sun, allowing for a deep, dark shadow to develop between the streets. After getting my bearings straight, I eventually push on like a great general in combat.

Then, out of the corner of my eye, a saint appears.

Dr. Rebecca Fraser, in her sporty red Mini Cooper, pulls up beside the road. Apparently, I haven't made it as far as I thought, maybe a half mile or so.

As the car's windows roll down, I dexterously perform a Slav squat in order to remain in eye contact.

"Where, uh, where are you going, Lawrence? You lost?" she says in a polite, yet sarcastic tone.

"I thought I'd take my suitcase, ol' Benji here, for a walk. He was cooped up inside the big, scary airplane for sixteen hours. You know how it goes," I say as I point toward my suitcase, trying to deflect any blame for losing my suitcase.

"Come on in. I'll take you back to the airport," she says.

"Wait. Wait. Wait. How'd you know I picked up the wrong bag?" I inquisitively reply.

"I do now. When I pulled up beside you, I saw that the tag said Wellington, not Lawrence. But thanks for confirming it."

Amazed at her keen eyesight, I eventually acquiesce, and I place ol' Benji inside of the compact trunk.

My apartment. She's a beaut, as they say Down Under.

She's on the thirty-second floor of some building whose name I can barely pronounce. However, the name isn't the point. She's still a beaut. She's a studio apartment with one bed and one bath and around three hundred square feet. As you walk through the front door, you are immediately greeted by a large abstract painting. I think it resembles either a horse or a spaceship. I do not possess an appreciation for art, much to the dismay of every liberal arts student. Moving through the front hallway, you are immediately greeted by a large Murphy bed in the middle of the room. Is there space for entertaining? Is there a proper kitchen? Will I even use the kitchen? These questions may have crossed your mind. The answer is very deep; the answer is a resounding *no*. You see, I'm a man of science, so socialization is forbidden through a complex set of rules and axioms developed by the "scientific elite."

The view, on the other hand, is spectacular. I opted for a smaller room in favor of a better view. My view is of the Brisbane River. It weaves throughout the central business district like a snake cutting through blades of grass. Although swimming is "frowned upon" by the local community (believe me, I asked), the river is the lifeblood of the community, transporting cargo and even military personnel in World War II.

Enough about glorified streams.

* * *

As I sit in my living room/bedroom/kitchen, I unpack my own creamsicle-tagged suitcase and realize I did not even bother to bring any cold weather clothes, not even a light jacket. Why? Because the team at AID assured me it was going to be relatively warm in Australia. For the most part, they are right, and it's a nice twenty degrees Celsius outside. However, the brochure for this place did not mention anything about "spontaneous trips to the Siberian Tundra."

Here's my dilemma: I am by no means a fashionista, but I do not think I will be able to wear a swimsuit in Siberia. I'm no expert in thermodynamics and hypothermia, but I think wearing shorts in cold weather is a very bad idea.

* * *

As the sun completes its twenty-four-hour life cycle, night turns into day, and Friday turns into Saturday—my day off. However, the serenity is soon spoiled, as I visualize an imaginary clock ticking down inside my head. I leave for Siberia, one of the coldest places on earth, in one week.

I struggle to gain the power to venture out of bed, and as a result I sit there motionless, watching mildly entertaining Facebook videos. Remember, I am a millennial. A hip one at that.

Eventually, after my willpower is restored through a poorly made cup of watered-down coffee, I finish my ablutions and dress myself in khaki shorts, a T-shirt, and flip flops (they call them "thongs" in Australia, but I don't want to taint your mind with anything promiscuous).

Feeling famished after my shower, I decide to make breakfast like a responsible adult would. However, considering that I just moved into my apartment last night, I don't have much food. You see, after Dr. Fraser and I adventured to the airport to rescue my bag, she dropped me off at my apartment at 7:00 p.m., and I crashed. Crossing the International Date Line really jumbles up your circadian rhythms, and it looks like mine are out of beat. No pun intended.

Because breakfast is ostensibly the "most important meal of the day" per my mother, I don my explorer cap once again and search for food—not merely a meager banana this time.

Dr. Lancaster did tell me yesterday that everything in Brisbane is walkable, so I figure, Why not get some exercise while looking for food?

I walk about two miles before I finally get to the city center with all of the boutique restaurants. The scenery is very reminiscent of yesterday. Large, modern buildings line the streets like trees line a game trail in the forest. Brisbane, as you may be able to tell, is a fairly modern and young city. True to Dr. Lancaster's synopsis, Brisbane is indeed walkable with bike and walking trails sprinkled throughout the city's densely packed business district. Contrary to my prior beliefs, Brisbane is dotted with several green spaces, which provide a nice bit a respite away from the hustle and bustle of the fast-paced business world.

After wandering the streets like a lost dog for fifteen minutes, I see a promising establishment. It's a boutique French café with another unpronounceable name, which can only mean one thing: it's either good or expensive. Although it's probably the latter, the gothic architecture seems inviting, and I eventually acquiesce and sit down at an open table.

My internal clock still believes that I'm on the East Coast of the United States, which is fourteen hours ahead. Because of this, I'm not craving a danish or a muffin. Oh no, I need a full buffet, and perhaps even a second buffet.

When I sit down, Damion, the waiter, immediately requests my order, and I just lay it on him. I order two appetizers, one entrée, three side dishes, and I'm pretty sure a salad manages to sneak in there too. In the past day and a half, I've only eaten Dr. Fraser's beloved banana and a meager airplane meal. I deserve this feast.

While I wait for my smorgasbord to arrive, I finally take time to relax. It is, after all, my day off.

Out of the corner of my eye, I notice a large TV levitating on the wall playing a news station—The Australian Broadcasting Corporation, I think?

After I pester Damion, he hands me the remote, so I guess I truly am the captain now.

I decide to leave it on the news, which is probably a shocker to most people. However, I think it's important to be immersed in the local political scene.

The words "Breaking News" are plastered across the screen as a fairly old, gray-haired news anchor starts giving a report on a currently evolving catastrophe.

"A large portion of eastern Australia is currently engulfed in flames. Although the cause of these fires remains unknown, the authorities are speculating that climate change may have a role in their intensity and their frequency. To elaborate on the issue, we have Dr. Timothy Michaels of the Department of the Environment. Dr. Michaels, how is climate change, this esoteric topic, causing these fires?"

"Well, climate change isn't really causing these fires; it is, however, increasing their intensity and their frequency. It can do this in a variety of ways, but the most common is rising temperatures. Australia has experienced some record temperatures in the past several months, peaking at 41.9 degrees Celsius. These temperatures, as we have seen in the past couple of years, have increased evaporation and decreased the amount of available water. As a result, these forests are literally drying up, and when you have a bunch of dried timber lining the forest floors, it can create a dangerous situation. All it takes is a spark."

"So, what you're saying is that the intensity is increasing because of all of this dried underbrush?" the news anchor says.

"Yes, but there really isn't a simple fix to the problem. You can't really *clean your forest floors.* It just doesn't work like that. You also have to worry about dead trees as well, which aren't as easy to remove. All of this creates a logistical nightmare for Australia as well as other nations," Dr. Michaels says.

"So, we have all of this dried debris, or leaf litter, covering the forest floors. What happens next in the cycle?" the news anchor inquires.

"Well, you need a spark. Now, climate change may potentially provide the spark through an increase in lightning strikes in the future; however, the jury is still out on that one. There is one very well-documented impetus of forest fires—and that's humans. Human-caused fires are the most destructive, primarily because they occur near population centres, and they are likely to increase in the future, as humans continue to push into nature."[3]

"Hooligans with matches. It's always a problem. Well, thank you for your time, Dr. Michaels. Now, the eastern Australian fires, which are predicted to burn up to seven million hectares, have already caused New South Wales and Queensland to declare states of emergency. Coming up, we'll tell you what that means for you," the news anchor says.

Just when I think the situation can't get any worse, I get a phone call from Dr. Lancaster on my day off. Being a doctor and getting a call on your day off is never a good sign.

"Hey, Dr. Lawrence, how's it going?"

I give him one of those corny replies like, "Never better, man."

---

3   Alejandra Borunda, "The Science Connecting Wildfires to Climate Change," *National Geographic*, September 17, 2020.

He then says, "We're going to have to shift around our schedule. There are forest fires burning throughout the eastern portion of Australia, and it's going to put a damper on our work at AID. As it stands now, you and Dr. Fraser are still slated to leave next Sunday, about a week from now. However, the declaration of emergency hampers things. We're going to need all hands on deck at the hospital because they're expecting a massive influx in patients in the coming days. As a result, I'm currently pulling the team from any ongoing projects for the next couple of days. Tomorrow, you need to meet the team at the Caboolture Hospital on McKean Street at 9 a.m."

Without hesitation, he hangs up on me before I can ask any questions and plead my case.

Not only is the world burning, but there's a potential pandemic brewing in Siberia. What a time to be alive.

Upon seeing me at a low point in my life, Damion quickly brings out my food.

I sit there, rib in hand, thinking about what clothes I need for Siberia.

As I walk outside of the French café, I notice my first problem: Australia is a relatively warm country most of the time. As a result, nobody really sells any cold-weather clothes, so this is going to be tough.

After pondering my options, I realize that I am a millennial, which means that I can do anything. I do what any tech-savvy person would do in this situation: I plan on ordering everything I need from Amazon, of course. Why would I waste my precious time looking for a haberdashery in this foreign land?

Unfortunately, I am sans my laptop at the moment, meaning I now have to walk back the full two miles to my apartment.

However, it is okay, because fitness is my passion, and it means that I can stop at the grocery store on the way back.

Upon returning to my humble abode, I immediately block out an hour to shop for the trendiest winter fashions, and my search does not take long. I find everything I need, and I even manage to stock up on some more of my kryptonite: barbecue sauce.

Thanks to Amazon, my order should, theoretically, be here in the coming days. Just in time for my not-so-serendipitous voyage to Siberia.

With no more chores for the rest of the day, I decide to follow up on the news anchor's discussion from earlier today. Dr. Michaels' explanation was sufficient, but it piqued my interest. As a result, I block out several hours to familiarize myself with this omnipresent phenomenon entangling Australia.

According to several prominent news sources, Australia is burning, and there are several ostensible causes. Sure, a deranged hooligan with a match could have started this fire, as the news anchor predicted, but that's unlikely. Additionally, a kangaroo plotting revenge on a koala could've started the fire, but again, that's unlikely. So where does that leave us? Well, the answer is simple: in my opinion, climate change is mostly to blame.

Let's break this down:

According to NASA, Earth's surface temperature has risen by about 1.62 degrees Fahrenheit in the past two hundred years. Big deal—what's the worst that could happen? Well, for starters, as Dr. Michaels explained, an increase in temperatures causes water to evaporate. That's what happens when you boil water; it's just a much more accelerated process in a pot. Plants, like humans, need water. Without water they die, and so do we. California and parts of Australia have, for the last several years, been under a historic drought, which has starved a lot of their trees, creating an environment rife with leaf litter and dead trees. Additionally, a starved tree is also a defenseless tree. Water is the lifeblood of a tree. Without water, it can't produce copious amounts of sap, which is what they use to seal their bark and protect against diseases. As a result, a tree that can't produce sap is much more susceptible to pests, like the bark beetle, and fungi. These droughts, as well as the prevalence of some pests, are expected to increase as the climate warms past 2.0 degrees Fahrenheit, which is why a considerable number of scientists are concerned for the future. In sum, Australia—she's thirsty.[4]

However, humans are also directly to blame for the forest fires, so climate change doesn't get all of the credit. Ever since the early 1900s, humans have practiced a policy of "any fire is a bad fire," and as a result, firefighters, under the auspices of politicians, have put out an exorbitant amount of fires, which has only exacerbated the prevalence of leaf litter. Fires are a natural occurrence, and they've been prevalent for thousands of years. In moderation, fires are beneficial for the environment, allowing seeds to fertilize and paving way for the next generation of trees. However, ever since humans have started to channel their inner Smokey the Bear, prematurely putting out or ending flames, forest fires have gotten much, much larger and more destructive.[5]

---

4   "Global Climate Change: Vital Signs of the Planet," National Aeronautics and Space Administration, Date Last Modified October 7, 2020.

5   Carol Miller, "The Hidden Consequences of Fire Suppression," *Park Science*, 28, (2012): 5-6.

The point to remember is this: anyone who tells you climate change is solely to blame for forest fires is not correct, and anyone who tells you climate change doesn't cause forest fires is also not correct. There's a delicate balancing act at play, and the scales are most likely going to tip in the future, leading to more frequent and more powerful fires.

Now, the cause of forest fires remains more abstruse. Lightning is a frequent cause; however, such fires are usually less destructive, as they occur out in the isolated wilderness. Humans are the most frequent cause of destructive fires. Humans have increased the development of housing communities, which has pushed humans' and forests' edges closer together. This Wildland-Urban Interface, as it's called in the science community, has been steadily expanding for the past several years, and it's a direct cause of forest fires. Somebody grilling in their backyard can cause a fire; a rogue, ill-advised gender reveal can cause a fire; or even a power line can cause a fire. The possibilities are endless, and that's the problem. It's impossible to predict where the next source of ignition is going to come from. As a result, we're at the mercy of a spontaneous, rapidly changing environment for the foreseeable future.[6]

Days pass, but I won't bore you with the particulars. All you need to know is that it's Monday.

You wouldn't believe what happened to me this morning.

---

6   Volker C. Radeloff et al., "Rapid Growth of the US Wildland-Urban Interface Raises Wildfire Risk," *Proceedings of the National Academy of Sciences, 115,* (March 2018): 5-6.

I was lying in my Murphy bed like Sleeping Beauty when all of a sudden, I heard a wailing alarm. At first, I was under the impression that it was my iPhone, but then I realized that nobody texts me in the first place. Something definitely went awry, so I set out to investigate. I stumbled through my apartment out into the main hall. The sound persisted and echoed, bouncing off the white walls and grey carpet. Then, I discovered the mystery: it was the fire alarm. The bright lights were repeatedly flashing, creating a rave-like effect. The building could've been on fire, so I decided to obey the posted placards and signage like a good boy. I deftly descended the building via the metal stairs, thirty-two flights and all.

While I was outside, I noticed something incredibly bizarre. The sky was and still is covered in a thick haze. This thick blanket of smoke reduced the visibility to less than one mile, and there was a fine film of soot lining everything. It was mysterious and eerie. It looked like a scene out of *The Walking Dead*: very ominous. The sun was supposed to be shining; it was 8:00 a.m. after all. However, you couldn't even see it. The sun merely produced a faint yellow and orange glow behind the layer of smoke.

I postulated that the haze was caused by forest fires in Sydney, but you can never be too sure nowadays. I didn't want to peddle fake news, so I decided to take a proactive approach. I asked one of the responding firefighters, a middle-aged man with a surprisingly well-kept handlebar mustache. To my surprise, he told me I was right. In fact, he also told me that the reason the fire alarm went off was because of smoke that must have seeped through an open window in the building. There wasn't even a fire. It was all a false alarm.

* * *

After the whole not-a-fire debacle, I returned to my domicile and freshened up before my big day at the hospital. It's now 8:57a.m. and I'm at the hospital, outside on the curb. Patients go in and out, and there's a faint wail of an ambulance siren in the distance. I'm early, for once. Dr. Lancaster never told me where to meet him, but I suspect that he meant outside. Now, I just have to wait for the rest of the gang to show up. A piece of cake if you ask me.

Several minutes go by, and nobody shows up.

I pace back and forth, whistling to pass the time. Concerned, I pull out my phone to check the time, and there's three missed calls from Dr. Lancaster.

Playing back the voicemails, I discover that I was supposed to meet the team in the first-floor conference room. This day keeps getting better and better.

* * *

Though I'm showing up several minutes late, Dr. Lancaster is still relatively happy to see me. I guess he thought I was going to bail and never come back. Trust me, that thought entered my mind a couple of times.

The meeting room is quite spacious, with four rows of black plastic and metal chairs. However, four chairs are already taken when I arrive: Dr. Lancaster, Dr. Fraser, and the dynamic duo whose names I do not remember.

"Alright ladies, gentlemen, and Dr. Lawrence. I, like many of you, would rather be in the lab right now. We have an emerging infectious disease on the horizon, and we have new cases of the Ebola and Crimean Congo Hemorrhagic Fever popping up in central Africa. This really isn't a good time for any of us; however, we are medical professionals with a duty to serve in a public health crisis," Dr. Lancaster says.

Then, Dr. Lancaster continues, "Let me break it all down. First, as you may know, most of Australia is burning, which has created a small public health crisis. Now, the fires are primarily located near Sydney and Melbourne, so we will most likely not see any burn victims today, which is good. However, as you probably noticed coming here, thick smoke currently blankets all of Brisbane. At first glance, this may not appear to be that bad; however, wood smoke is unique. Not only does it contain fine particulate matter, ranging from ten micrometers all the way down to 2.5 micrometers, but it also contains known carcinogens. Now, these particles can find their way into the upper respiratory tract and the lungs, causing a lot of bad things. They can get into the blood stream if they're small enough, or they can cause an excess amount of mucus to build up in the lungs, leading to respiratory problems. Because of this, we are expecting an uptick in the number of hospital visits in the coming days for respiratory conditions, asthma, ophthalmologic problems, and even mental health problems. Your task today and for the rest of the week is to help out in any way, shape, or form. If they need you to do anything, you do it. Now, if there are any questions, you can direct them to Dr. Howard here. He's on the hospital staff and has been put in charge of this whole operation."

"Dr. Howard, what subset of the population are vulnerable to these forest fires?" says Dr. Fraser.

"Well, it's tough to say right now. However, firefighters are our primary concern, considering their preexisting history of smoke inhalation. Other vulnerable groups are young children, people with preexisting conditions like asthma, and smokers. The science isn't quite there yet, but we may also see an uptick in visits from people with cardiovascular problems. Treatment is pretty much going to depend on which subset of the population we're dealing with. If they have preexisting asthma, you might want to use an inhaled corticosteroid or a quick relief inhaler. The primary goal for you all, considering your unique research-oriented backgrounds, is not going to be hands-on today. You're merely going to assist in any way you can. As a result, I would deflect any treatment questions to the attending physician."

"Dr. Howard, how are the fires going to impact the health of the population months down the line? It seems like we're merely dealing with the quick response and not so much on the chronic aspect of the fires."

"Dr. Lawrence, that's a very great question. The research isn't quite there, as most studies focus merely on the short-term effects of wildfire smoke; however, preliminary studies have linked an increase in wildfire smoke to an increase in influenza cases months after the initial fire, so we may see an uptick in respiratory infections a couple months from now. Like I said, the exact mechanism isn't well understood, but we do know a stressful situation can weaken the immune system, making you more susceptible to infections later on."[7]

"Wow. Alright then. Thank you for that, Dr. Howard."

At that moment, Dr. Howard's name is called on the intercom, and he cordially excuses himself from the meeting room.

---

7   Erin Landguth et al., "The Delayed Effect of Wildfire Season Particulate Matter on Subsequent Influenza Season in a Mountain West Region of the USA," *Environment International* 139, (June 2020): 5-6.

"Alright, if that's everything, then this meeting is dismissed. Now, go help out where you're needed," says Dr. Lancaster.

* * *

Well, several hours have passed, and the day has turned into night.

It was a busy day, but I'll try to give a brief synopsis of what happened.

First, after the meeting ended, I wandered the halls.

After my initial search proved fruitless, I found a room with a young kid who suffered from asthma. My new friend, Max, told me his asthma usually wasn't that bad; however, the increased smoke inhalation wreaked havoc on his respiratory tract. Like Dr. Howard and Dr. Lancaster mentioned, the particulate matter, specifically 2.5 microns or fewer, can seep into the lungs, causing a reaction. The lungs secrete a mucus in an effort to coat the foreign particulate matter; however, this decreases the efficiency of the lungs, leading to respiratory problems, which is what happened to Max. He was a sweetheart though, and he even gave me his Jell-O.

After I had a discussion with Max about the intricacies of interstellar space travel, I was called to a different room. To my surprise, I stumbled upon a very nice, middle-aged lady whose name was Sarah. Her case was quite unique: she suffered from PTSD. Strange? I know. She regaled me with stories about how when she was little her house burned down, and I guess the smell of the smoke must have triggered her PTSD. It's strange, because I thought I would've only dealt with patients who suffered from physical health complications, not mental ones. I guess the world is changing, for the worse.

What worries me is that this is just the beginning. As Dr. Howard said, when the body experiences a stressful situation, like having your house burned from a forest fire or losing a family member during a severe hurricane, it usually diverts energy away from crucial bodily functions. For instance, stress is known to trigger an immune suppression wherein the body produces fewer lymphocytes, a crucial part of the body's immune system. As a result, with an increasing frequency of forest fires and other environmental extremes likely in the future, our bodies will be less effective at fighting off deadly pathogens, leading to an increased infectivity of infectious diseases.[8]

Because of our overwhelming success on the first day, the AID team and I plan on spending the next couple of days at the hospital, helping in any way we can. Hopefully that means more free Jell-O.

When all is said and done, I'll be leaving for Siberia. What could go wrong?

---

8   David G. Meyers and C. Nathan DeWall, *Exploring Psychology in Modules* (New York: Worth Publishers, 2019), 389.

CHAPTER 3

OFF TO SIBERIA

It's 7:40 a.m.

I wake up to a bright light shining through the porous white linen curtains of my apartment. It isn't Jesus saving me from going to Siberia. Far from it, actually. Perturbed by the incessant beam of unidentified light burning a metaphorical hole in my retinas, I decide to crawl out of bed and begin my morning rituals.

I slick back the curtains, and the full wrath of the sun's powerful rays hit me like a freight train. I stand there, absorbing the warmth and most definitely dangerous UV radiation. After my eyes adjust to the blinding light, I see nothing special (to me): just the weaving and winding of the Brisbane River as well as some cars crossing a bridge whose name I do not know.

Feeling satisfied by the daily dose of cosmic radiation, I begin the arduous journey of packing my bags for Siberia; we are, after all, leaving today.

I festoon my queen-sized bed with a plethora of clothes, accoutrements, and other accessories that one might find in a haberdashery: a long, wooden shoe horn (thick rubber boots are hard to put on), a bright red power tie (if I end up discovering the next big one, I will probably be invited to some galas with the president of the United States or the PM of Australia, so who knows?), and the *pièce de résistance*: lots of barbecue sauce (no explanation needed).

Of course, there are other things thrown into the pile as well—rain jackets, other cold weather gear, and toilet paper (an essential when you're spending a couple of weeks in a foreign environment). However, I decide to forgo the luxuries on this one. No Gucci flip flops, no messenger bags, and, most importantly, no drip.

I don't how long I'm going to be gone, but I don't think spontaneous return voyages from Siberia are all that cheap or common. Come to think of it, I don't think anyone's ever come back from Siberia. It really makes you think . . .

Now comes the hard part: I have to pack my entire wardrobe for both Australia and Siberia into three reasonably sized suitcases, which should be enough clothes to last me for a couple hours or weeks, depending on how adventurous I feel wearing khakis.

I will spare the gruesome details, but all you need to know is that after much tribulation, I eventually conquer the impossible and manage to fill every nook and cranny of the suitcases.

With the suitcases bulging in every direction like a packrat's storage unit, I decide to indulge in some breakfast, or "brekkie" as they call it down under. Nothing too fancy; I'm still on a budget. Sitting at the kitchen table (it's really my desk and my countertop all in one), I prepare the finest of frozen waffles served with genetically modified syrup mixed with copious amounts of corn syrup. The cardboard-like texture of the frozen waffles balances out the sliminess and stickiness of the molasses-colored syrup. It's not a full-fledged English breakfast, but the last time I was on a plane for several hours, I almost starved. This time, I'm not taking any chances.

With a belly full of frozen waffles and a full box of Tim Tams, I decide to pack up my backpack, filling it with my laptop, a couple of last-minute essentials, and this time, my headphones.

Like a college kid being evicted from his parents' house, I dexterously glide the three cumbersome suitcases out into the carpeted hall, accidentally scratching and denting every wall in sight.

Satisfied, I close the door to my apartment for the last time. A loud creaking sound envelops the hall, and I proceed to the elevator.

* * *

I meet Dr. Fraser and Dr. Lancaster in the lobby.

They're sitting across from each other in rigid-looking grey chairs, occupying a sitting area nearest the bathrooms. They must have heard the elevator ding, because as soon as I arrive in the lobby, they immediately stand up like anxious meerkats monitoring a threat. I am the (ostensible) threat.

They both fixate their attention at me, potentially judging my travel attire: Crocs, socks, and sweatpants with a Metallica tee. The austere Dr. Fraser is merely wearing blue jeans with a light gray jacket, presumably of the bargain brand, and hiking boots.

Trying to lighten the mood and usurp the power in the situation, I ask, "How's it going, lady and gentleman?"

"You know you're late, Dr. Lawrence. Right?" says Dr. Lancaster, aka the chief of the punctuality police.

"Really? I don't own a watch, nor can I read one. I prefer to use island time. It purportedly reduces stress." I deftly wave my hands in the air to articulate my point.

"Um, Lawrence, what's that on your wrist?" says Dr. Fraser.

"Rebecca, my *eyes* are up here," I reply.

They both let out an audible groan, and I crown myself victorious.

With the mood spoiled, we walk through the glass lobby and through the electric sliding doors over to Dr. Lancaster's Land Rover Defender underneath the massive concrete awning covering the circular drive. Dr. Lancaster's truck is quite spacious, and it manages to stow not only my three bags but also Dr. Fraser's four bags.

Back in the lobby I called shotgun, but I was overruled because of Dr. Fraser's seniority. So, I was relegated to the caboose, next to the mountainous tower of luggage.

With a slam of the trunk and the backfire of an engine, we depart, weaving our way through the wide streets of Brisbane's Central Business District on our way to the airport.

Although I feel like a caged-in animal in a foreign meat market, I eventually settle in. Dr. Lancaster starts briefing us on our voyage.

"Alright, I hope you two both know you are headed to Novosibirsk, Siberia," he says.

Yeah, I wish we were going to Cabo, but . . .

"You two will meet up with Alexi, who is our liaison provided by the Russian government. Speaking of the Russian government, they haven't told us anything. We haven't received our samples yet, and you two are going to be the first outsiders into the country to study this thing. Anyway, this is what we know, given the present information: last week, we received a call from the Russian Centres for Disease Control about a possible outbreak of some pathogen. It could be viral; it could be bacterial; it could be a prion; hell, we don't even know. All they have said is that they've quarantined a ten-mile radius around where the first index case was identified, so you two should, hopefully, be the first people on scene," he says.

I'm not a big fan of lectures. I'm more of a learn-on-the-fly kind of guy, so I just gaze out the rectangular window at the passing scenery. Man, am I going to miss this place.

"That's where you can find the instructions," he says.

Whoops. I must have missed something, but Dr. Fraser is the leader and not me, so . . .

"Your job is to figure out what we're dealing with and report back to me. You'll have most of the necessary tools, and anything you can't do—stuff like electron microscopy and viral culturing—send it back to the lab here and we will take care of that," says Dr. Lancaster.

"So, we're basically the guinea pigs who are tasked with getting the samples from the belly of the beast?" I ask.

"The job you two are doing is incredibly important, Dr. Lawrence. You have the potential to thwart an outbreak. Don't mess it up," he says.

Great! Just what I wanted.

"Oh, the AID team has also sent supplies and machines up to Novosibirsk, so once you end up at the final location, you can do some—simpler—on-site testing," says Dr. Lancaster.

I ask, "For real, do we have any idea of what's going on?"

"No. They haven't given us anything—no samples, nothing. So, we'll be working from the ground up. All we know is that it's apparently new," says Dr. Lancaster.

"How long are we going to be up there?" asks Dr. Fraser.

"I don't know. It could be three, four . . ." says Dr. Lancaster.

"Days?" I ask.

" . . . weeks, or three to four months, maybe. Depending on how fast you work," says Dr. Lancaster.

I could potentially spend the next three to four months in the backwoods of Siberia. When I wanted to study medicine, this was not what I had in mind.

After Dr. Lancaster's eye-opening answer, the mood of the car shifts and the conversation stalls.

The sound of Dr. Lancaster's twenty-year-old Defender creates ominous white noise, like a gentle hum.

Unfortunately, there's only one thing I can do to break the silence: I can spout utter nonsense for the rest of the car ride.

"So, hypothetically, if we discover that it's a new pathogen—let's say a virus—who gets to name it?"

"What?" says Dr. Lancaster.

Dr. Fraser turns around in her seat and gives me her famous look with a tilt of the head and a squint of the eyes. She's either so enthused with my inquisitive behavior, or she thinks I'm a complete moron.

"Well, you know, if this thing turns out to be a new, novel virus, who gets to name it? This is, of course, all in the hypothetical."

I manage to stump Dr. Lancaster and Dr. Fraser. My philosophical question leaves them speechless.

"Because I came up with a list of pretty cool names. I created a spreadsheet last night. Do y'all want to hear them?"

"You know, Dr. Lawrence, why don't we leave the naming to the International Committee on Taxonomy of Viruses. They've done a good job in the past. More importantly, not to be indecorous or anything, but I don't want you naming it something offensive," says Dr. Lancaster, aka the killer of my creativity.

"I would never," I gasp. "I know the rules and regulations."

"I'm sure you do, Dr. Lawrence. I'm sure you do. . . ."

* * *

When we reach the airport Dr. Lancaster helps us unload our bags and some of our equipment, and then he does what any boss would do: he unenthusiastically says goodbye and quickly absconds.

"Well, goodbye, guys. See you soon. Oh, also, don't bring back whatever that thing is. We don't need a pandemic on our hands," says Dr. Lancaster as he drives off.

I wanted a kiss goodbye, but we don't always get what we want in life.

Here we are. Like two peas in a pod. Like a true dynamic duo. Like fire and ice.

Dr. Fraser immediately takes charge, fearing that I may lead our voyage astray.

Upon clearing security, we head to the gate to wait to board our ridiculously long flight to Moscow.

When we finally sit down at gate twenty-one, Dr. Fraser starts peppering me with questions.

At least it's not silence.

"Do you want to go get snacks?" says Dr. Fraser.

"Ya, of course. I'd *love* to spend thirty dollars on a bag of pretzels and water."

"I think you're forgetting about my banana and my interest payments."

"How could I forget about your beloved banana? You know, I'm pretty sure I did you a favor."

"Oh, yeah? How so, Lawrence?"

"Hey, I don't need to explain myself. This isn't the *Dr. Lawrence Explains Gameshow.*"

"That's what I thought."

Immediately after I find an empty row of seats, we are off again. My life is an adventure, that's for sure. As we walk into the small kiosk, I immediately notice something that catches my eye.

No, it's not food. You know, I'm not hungry all the time.

Hidden in a wall of magazines, like a needle in a haystack, is an intriguing magazine by my favorite media company, the *National Geographic.* On front of the cover is a very artistic shot of a penguin, dressed in its usual black and white. The front cover is what interests me; it's the simple and enigmatic title: "The Victims of Climate Change."

As I pick up the flimsy, paper magazine, Dr. Fraser swoops in a hawklike fashion.

"Wow, I didn't know you read!" says Dr. Fraser.

"Nah. I'm more of a pretty picture person. They say a picture is worth a thousand words, Rebecca."

"Cute," she replies as she gives me a very forced smile.

Fortunately, Rebecca becomes distracted like a cat chasing a laser and she runs off, leaving me alone.

After browsing a multitude of options, I, like any normal person, decide to buy the *Nat Geo* magazine, a water, and more Tim Tams. Dr. Fraser, on the other hand, buys vegan health bars and kale chips. A recipe for disaster, if you ask me. As I'm about to pay, she, again, swoops in and pays for me.

"Woah there. I'm a big boy. I got this," I reply.

"That's cute, but Dr. Lancaster wants me to keep track of every purchase for reimbursement purposes."

"So, wait. You're telling me that I could've bought anything I wanted, no matter how expensive it was?"

"And that's why he put me in charge."

"It's only a hypothetical question."

We eventually return to our seats, which are, to my surprise, still empty. The seats provide a great view of the tarmac through the tall and wide windows. Planes pull in and out, creating a chaotic environment.

In an attempt to strike up a typical conversation, I start talking about the weather.

"Beautiful day out. No clouds in the sky. It's sort of like . . ."

"You never bought me a banana," Dr. Fraser butts in.

"Rebecca, I think we may have a bigger problem on our hands than a banana. There's a potential pandemic brewing in the motherland, penguins are apparently dying, and you bought kale chips, which is a problem in and of itself."

Sitting there dumbfounded at my ignorance toward kale, Dr. Fraser replies, "They're a healthy alternative to potato-based chips, and they happen to contain several vitamins and minerals."

"I'm pretty sure a lot of things contain vitamins and minerals, Rebecca."

"What's your problem with kale chips anyway?"

"It's a complicated story," I reply.

"We have all the time in the world," she says.

"Alright. I may be a man of the sciences, but I'm also a man of the markets. The stock markets, that is. In the past several months, I have heavily invested my hard-earned money in the stock markets. Now, picture this: a dashing, young doctor with nothing better to do with his money. What did I do? Do I buy a Ferrari? Do I purchase an alpaca? No. I invested it. I am smart. 'Where?' you might ask, but that's beside the point. The point is that I didn't invest in kale, and I'm pissed at the kale marketing boom.

I could've made so much money. I would have *kaled* it. No pun intended. . . ."

She rolls her green eyes in agony and begins to speak.

"W-w-wait, I haven't finished yet. My dissatisfaction with kale stems from the fact that kale is disgusting," I continue.

"So you're a licensed medical doctor who doesn't like healthy foods?" she replies.

"Yes. Yes I am."

"Hmmm . . ." She stares off in another direction, people watching to pass the time.

An awkward silence develops.

"I'll be back," I say.

"Wait, where are you going?" she says as I walk away.

Leaving my bag with Dr. Fraser is a risk, but it's a one I'm willing to take.

I wander. I wander all throughout the terminal, observing the kitschy objects in each of the stores. Would you like a pink Brisbane-scented candle? Whatever that might entail.

I eventually circle back from my peregrination and begin checking on our flight information on the giant flatscreens.

In big block letters, it says "BRISBANE TO MOSCOW: DELAYED BECAUSE OF WEATHER," or something like that. The font is blurry, and my eyes are frail.

Concerned, I go check in with the gate agent, a young female, maybe in her early thirties, like Dr. Fraser.

"How's it going, sir?" she asks.

"It's splendid. Well, it was splendid. You see, my flight from Brisbane to Moscow is, unfortunately, delayed. What's going on, if I may ask?"

"Well, the control tower and the pilots say there's bad weather over Malaysia right now."

"Really?"

"Yes. Who would've thought?" she replies.

"Well, I took a class in college about weather dynamics."

Sensing my sarcasm, she replies, "I bet you did," as she smiles.

"Well, actually, yes. You see, Malaysia has quite a unique climate. It's hot, like all other equatorial climates, of course, but that's not what makes it interesting. Rather, it's the rainfall. Malaysia gets, on average, ninety-eight inches in a year, with the eastern region getting a monstrous two hundred inches in a year. Quite a lot, if you ask me. Now, my plane serendipitously happens to be leaving right at the tail-end of Malaysia's Southwest Monsoon season. What are the chances? Because of this factoid, I would have originally assumed that a monsoon was the cause of our delay. So, to answer your question: I would have thought that. Now, I'm not a pilot, an aviation enthusiast, or a weather boy, but I don't think big metal tubes, water, and electricity mix that well. That's why the ground crew has advised against an on-time departure."

"Oh . . . well . . . thank you for the presentation on precipitation," she awkwardly replies.

"Yeah, the more you know," I say as I wave goodbye.

I weave my way in and out of the large crowds assembling outside of a rival gate until I finally reach our gate, gate twenty-one, at the end of the terminal.

"Where'd you go?" Dr. Fraser asks as I sit down.

"Saw some things. Made quite an impression on our gate agent."

"That is a very vague and unconvincing response. What things? What agent?" she asks.

"You know. Candles and stuff," I reply.

Dr. Fraser shakes her head, throwing it back. "What? Candles?"

"Candles. Pink ones. And I gave a lesson about the weather to our gate agent."

"What are you saying?" she says, becoming confused.

"You know. I talked to the gate agent about Malaysia's geography and weather patterns."

"Was it warranted? Did she want to know about the weather?" she inquires.

"Well, she asked a question," I reply.

"What question did she ask?"

"She said 'Who would've thought?' so I gave her an answer of 'who would've thought.'"

Dr. Fraser bends down in the chair and puts her head in her hands, letting out an audible groan.

"Lawrence! That's a rhetorical question. You're not supposed to answer it."

"Really? I guess I really don't have emotional intelligence. *Who would've thought*?" I say as I smirk. "Anyway, the information screens said that the flight is delayed by about an hour, which means that you have to spend an extra hour with me. *Don't you feel invigorated yet?*"

She looks me directly in the eyes and says nothing.

"What? Do I have something in my teeth? Oh man, you should've told me."

"No, it's not that. Why are you like that?" she says.

"Like what?"

"You're clearly smart, yet when people try and decipher who you really are, you portray yourself as, for lack of a better word, a goofball."

"A goofball? That's a new term. Where'd you look that up? Dictionary dot com?"

"You're doing it again!"

"What? Being irresistibly attractive?"

"You're getting defensive. It's like you don't want me to know why."

"What seat are you in, Rebecca?"

"I'm in 6B."

"That's fine. I'm in 6A, which is, if I'm correct, first class. I guess the Russian government spared no expense. It might be a bribe, but I'm not complaining."

"Don't change the subject. Why are you like that?"

"Like I said earlier. This isn't the *Dr. Lawrence Explains Gameshow.*"

"We have a sixteen-hour flight ahead of us, and we have more travel time on top of that. If I want to know the answer, I'll find it."

As I stuff my face with my fifth Tim Tam, I say, "Yeah, but I'm pretty sure it's almost your afternoon nap time, so good luck with that, Rebecca."

She looks at her watch, presumably to check the veracity of my statement, and she lets out an audible sigh.

* * *

Thirty minutes later our plane finally lands. Then the behemoth of a plane slowly pulls into its glorified parking spot, and the ground crews immediately spring into action.

Dr. Fraser is already starting to drift into a weary, nap-like state. I guess I was right.

"Wakey wakey, eggs and bakey, sleepy head."

"What is wrong with you, Lawrence?"

"Plane's here. Let's go!" We start to pack up our belongings that are strewn across the floor.

* * *

Upon entering the Aeroflot 777, we are immediately escorted to our seats, 6A and 6B.

I'll tell you something: the Russians know something about style. The seats are more spacious than Dr. Fraser's purse, and there are nooks and crannies with all sorts of little goodies. I even find a little pouch with free socks.

I ask, "What time is it?"

"Don't you have a watch?" she replies.

"Is that a rhetorical question? I'm still learning the whole socialization thing, remember?"

"Oh, dear," she lets out a gasp. "I'm in for a long flight."

"Do you think they'll serve food?"

"What is with you and food all of the time? Do you want any of my kale chips?"

"No thanks. I guess I'll just starve again."

Meanwhile, I sit there, like a kid in the candy store, unpacking all my goodies and playing with my seat.

I pass the time by staring out the large, ovoid-shaped window, admiring the cracks in the concrete tarmac. Several minutes go by, and the rest of the passengers eventually file in like sardines.

The cabin crew dims the lights and begin welcoming the first-class passengers in their seats. Then, a metaphorical angel from heaven appears. One of the chief stewardesses offers me a menu replete with the finest of luxuries: food, and lots of it.

When I turn to ask Dr. Fraser what she's going to eat, she's already asleep. I guess some people aren't meant for the hustle and bustle of air travel.

* * *

While we are in the air, I decide to indulge in not one but two entrées. I am not about to let Dr. Fraser's meal go to waste.

My chicken comes anointed with the finest of creamy mushroom sauces, and my steak is delivered at a beautiful medium temperature (the only way to eat a steak). Normally, airplane meals are served in an aluminum, or some other flimsy metal receptacle; however, like I said earlier, the Russians know a thing or two about style, and my meal comes delivered on the finest of plates with silver cutlery on either side.

Sitting there like a king in a castle, I ruminate on what might lie ahead.

Let me just say, for the record, I think this expedition is a very, very bad idea.

Here's the reason why I think it's a bad idea. First off, it happened in a very remote part of Siberia, which in and of itself is bad. What happens if Dr. Fraser or I get infected? Where's the nearest hospital? There is not one. To make matters worse, the Russians clearly haven't given us the whole story there. This thing could be a bioweapon, or it could be the next influenza.

Now, let me be clear for a second: I do not think the Russians created a bioweapon; however, governments have, in recent years, decided that it is in their best will to quietly squash outbreaks before the mainstream media becomes aware. It's better for the governments to hide it. They can save face more easily. If word got out that the Russians knew about this for several weeks and did nothing, their economy would tank, and their political capital would diminish. Some nations are more proactive than others, so we will see.

The point is I don't like where this is going.

After fifteen hours and a six thousand-calorie food coma, I wake up to Dr. Fraser logging her past day into a leather-bound journal.

"Wow, wait a minute. Is that a diary? Dr. Fraser, I am flabbergasted."

"Um. No. It's a journal. I'm calculating how much interest you owe me on my banana, and let's just say that pretty soon you're going to owe me a full meal."

"Please. I've dealt with more threatening bookies. Anyway, how much time do we have left?"

"About thirty minutes or so."

As our plane glides through the haze, buildings start to emerge—it's Moscow with its typical Communist-era concrete buildings near the airport. Additionally, my initial premonitions were, in fact, wrong: there is no snow on the ground. It turns out that Russia, like most places, is not covered in snow all year round. Who knew?

* * *

After we land in Moscow, we head to baggage claim, which is surprisingly swanky. The floor's white tiles blend nicely with the industrial look of the baggage claim.

As we wait for our bags, we start looking around for our chaperone in the maze of people.

"Rebecca, whom are we looking for again?"

"Dr. Lancaster said something about a man named Alexi."

"Alrighty then," I say as I pick up our bags from the motorized conveyor belt.

With our bags in hand, we begin the arduous journey of playing human-sized *Where's Waldo?*

It doesn't take us long, and we finally notice him.

"Rebecca, is that him?" I ask.

"I guess so. He has a sign that says our names," she replies.

"Yeah, but he looks like a lumberjack, not a scientist. Are you sure?" I reply.

There's nothing wrong with a scientist who may moonlight as a lumberjack. I've just never seen one before, and I'm a bit skeptical.

Alexi is quite a scruffy looking man, standing alone in the corner with a petite sign that says, "Doctor Fraser and Lawrence: AID."

He's built like a tree—six foot three inches and weighing about 250 pounds. He is, unironically, wearing a flannel button-down shirt with jeans and the Russian brand of Timberlands. To put the icing on the cake, his beard is unkempt yet stylish. I think he might coif it. Not sure.

As we approach him, he speaks to us in a thick Russian accent:

"Are you Dr. Lawrence and Dr. Fraser from Australia?"

We both nod our heads in unison.

"Wonderful. Please come. We are heading to your airplane."

Intrigued, yet scared, I reply:

"Our plane? Like a private plane?"

"Yes, yes. The Russian government chartered a plane for the AID team to take to Novosibirsk. We want you on the ground as soon as possible."

Dr. Fraser and I raise our eyebrows at each other. Can it be? Are we going in style again?

Alexi shows us to his car—a red, four-doored Lada Granta. He even offers to stow our bags in the trunk. I'm not sure how it's going to fit, but he's still a gentleman.

"So, doctors, how was the flight?" he says as he closes the driver's door.

"Yeah, it was a fun one, Alexi. I got to eat two meals at once because Dr. Fraser over here prefers kale chips to a steak. Can you believe that, Alexi?"

"In Russia, we do not believe in kale."

"That's my man. What do Russians 'believe' in then?"

"Vodka, and lots of it."

At this point, Dr. Fraser and I both start to smell the faint whiff of alcohol on his clothes. Now, I may not be Mr. Righteous (I did purloin Dr. Fraser's banana), but I don't think alcohol and machinery mix that well.

After hearing that, we hastily fasten our seatbelts and cling onto the door.

* * *

Eventually, we arrive at the "private" terminal we were promised.

"*Voilà!* Isn't she beautiful?" says Alexi.

"I'm sorry? Where is it? Is it behind the cargo plane?" says Dr. Fraser.

"No. No. No. This is your private plane. It's very nice. It's an Ilyushin Il 76. Isn't she beautiful? Built in 1974. It was one of the first ones off the assembly line. Very safe airplane."

My man, Alexi, wants us to get on this decrepit relic from the Soviet Union. I mean, the plane is older than I am.

"Alexi, man. What happened to our private airplane? I pictured something a little newer and nicer."

"She'll be fine. Novosibirsk is too far for the small private plane. Also, you have a lot of equipment. It's too heavy for a small plane. We have to improvise," he says.

Alexi is right. The massive, four-engine plane should be able to hold our six suitcases and the humongous shipping container of equipment that Dr. Lancaster sent from the AID headquarters. I'm just disappointed. That's all.

As we board the rust bucket via a rusted metal ladder, I immediately say a prayer. I'm not even that religious.

The interior of the plane is not for the faint of heart. There are exposed wires dangling from the ceiling, and there are missing panels on the wall. To make matters worse, it smells of gasoline and rust, sort of like a deep country gas station on a Tuesday afternoon. I guess the Russian government did spare an expense in this instance.

Upon sitting down in the lone row of chairs near the front of the cargo bay, I immediately begin toying with the forty-year-old plane: playing with random switches and opening the window shades.

When I look over at Dr. Fraser, I notice she's frantically trying to fasten her makeshift seatbelt.

"Having fun there, Rebecca?"

"I'm a little nervous. I read an article about one of these that went down in 2016 fighting a forest fire, and the whole crew died."

"Well, if we go down, at least we'll be buried together, like an old married couple," I chuckle.

Predictable Dr. Fraser remains unamused.

Annoyed that her seat belt will not fasten, she goes to check on Alexi and the flight crew instead.

Meanwhile, I try to look busy by intently watching a large black bird, maybe a crow, through a cracked window.

Then, I hear it:

"Dr. Lawrence, get up here!"

Oh great, they found my secret stash.

I quickly run up to the flight deck, trying to explain myself.

"I know what you may be thinking, but I need it. A man's got to chill once in a while."

"What are you talking about, Lawrence?" says Dr. Fraser.

They didn't find my suitcase filled with barbecue sauce. We're good for now.

"Nothing. I got distracted."

"Okay. So the flight will take about four hours or so. Right now, you guys can relax in the main cargo bay. I'll be up here if you need me," says Alexi.

Oh how the mighty have fallen. I, Dr. Lawrence, was the king of the sky, flying in first class like Icarus, and now, I've flown too close to the sun.

Returning to the cargo bay, Dr. Fraser and I sit back down in the rusted-metal and burlap seats, facing the back of the airplane.

In a moment's notice, the airplane's four engines come to life, filling the cabin with a cacophony of noises, vibrations, and smells—lots of peculiar smells.

With another four hours of flight time and several more hours of travel ahead, Dr. Fraser and I do the only right thing to do: we sleep.

Dr. Fraser and I both awake to severe turbulence. The seats start to rattle, and the exposed wires in the ceiling start to sway back and forth.

At first, I think nothing of it, but then Dr. Fraser reminds me that Alexi may or may not be intoxicated. Concerned for our lives, we immediately spring up and investigate. We gracefully waddle through the narrow passageway toward the cockpit and pry open the door.

"Alexi!" I yell. "What's going on, my man?"

"Oh, it's nothing. Just a little bit of rough air. We should be landing very, very soon."

"How long is very, very soon?" says Dr. Fraser.

Alexi speaks some inaudible Russian to the pilots.

"The pilot says we have about ten minutes left, so go buckle up."

Following Alexi's mandate, we both return to our improvised seats next to the ovoid window.

"Rebecca, if we make it out of here alive, I'm so done with flying. I'll take trains or something like that."

"That's technically impossible in a modern society. Because we have become so reliant on air travel for transportation, you would be alienating yourself in an ever-progressing society. You'd be much better off flying in a plane that wasn't built forty years ago."

"You're no fun. Just let me imagine."

To pass the time, I stare out the window, admiring the picturesque countryside: it's not like Australia.

There are almost no buildings, only trees. For miles and miles, spruce and cypress trees dot the landscape without a road in sight. It really is nature in its pristine form—without human interaction.

* * *

The plane eventually lands, and Alexi drops another bombshell on us.

"Welcome to Novosibirsk, Siberia. Now, the camps are a couple of hours outside the city, and they are off road. We will have to take SUVs in order to get there."

Alexi and I start loading the crates of equipment into SUV's trunk and the attached trailer.

"I'm sorry. Did you say camps?"

You see, it's a valid question. Back in Russia's Communist days, they had labor camps, and I'm a doctor, not a historian, so I have to clarify.

"Yes, camps," he replies.

"Well, what types of camps?"

"Ivory camps. It's where they mine for ivory from woolly mammoths. It's a small scale operation, but they have had some problems with a pathogen."

Dr. Fraser and I both become silent, and we just stare at each other, pondering the mess that we're about to embark on.

* * *

While in the car with Alexi, Dr. Fraser and I start to piece together what actually happened.

"So, Alexi, my man. What exactly happened at these camps?"

"Well, it's a long story, but we have a four-hour car ride, so I can try to explain."

"Hit it," I say.

"Okay, let me provide some backstory about the woolly mammoth in Siberia. First, Russia has one of the largest concentrations of frozen woolly mammoths in the world, with millions buried in the permafrost. The last woolly mammoth was alive around four thousand years ago, but the majority of mammoths found in Siberia were living around ten thousand years ago. It's interesting because humans lived at the same time, and we think that humans may have interacted with the mammoths, but we're not quite sure yet. Anyway, when these mammoths died from natural causes, like floods or diseases, they were buried under a layer of permafrost and mud. This layer created something like a tomb, encapsulating the mammoth. Because of this, Russia has some of the best preserved mammoths in the world. Scientists at local universities are keen to study these mammoths. However, problems have arisen."

Alexi becomes silent. It's as if he isn't supposed to reveal the whole story.

"What types of problems?" Dr. Fraser asks.

"In the past couple of years, some parts of the permafrost did not even freeze. In the summer months, Siberia temperature can get in the hundreds, making it easier for the permafrost to thaw. These increased temperatures are raising the rate at which our permafrost thaws. This creates problems. For instance, many, many woolly mammoths have been found because the dirt and thawed permafrost just wash away. As a result, there are people who trek out to the forest in order to mine these tusks for profit. Now, some obtain a license and are approved by the government to dig for mammoths for research purposes. However, the majority of camps are illegal operations. They dig up these tusks with the goal of selling them on the black market. It's a very bad business. It creates an environmental problem."

"Well, who's buying these tusks?" I ask.

"Many, many people. The Chinese are a big buyer as well as other east Asian countries. You know, it's sort of an 'ethical ivory' because it died thousands of years ago. There is no killing. They use it for all sorts of things, but I don't want to get into specifics."

"Okay, but who found the camp, and how did they find it?" Dr Fraser asks.

"Well, in Russia, we take our environmental protection very seriously, so we have many, many patrols on the river. These environmental protection officers enforce the law and confiscate the finds of hunters without a license."

"So why do you need doctors?"

"This is where it gets complicated. About two weeks ago, we dispatched one of our routine environmental patrols. Most of the time, the tuskers, as they are called, throw tarps and netting over their equipment in order to camouflage it from our patrols. However, on this patrol, the officers found a campsite. It was very suspicious because the boats were still docked, and all the equipment was plugged in. However, when the officers searched the surrounding area, they found several dead bodies. We don't know how the men died. At first, we thought it was a rival camp who did it, but the men did not show any signs of a struggle. When the officers reported their findings, we dispatched another crew. However, we were never able to locate the original patrol. We found the boat, but we don't know where they went. We don't know if it is a virus, a bacterium, or something like that."

"So has anyone been to the camp after the original patrol? Did the second patrol make it to the camp?" asks Dr. Fraser.

"No. The second patrol drove by on the boat and tried to contact the crew via radio. No one responded. Then we called the Russian CDC, and they asked the AID team for help."

"Wait a minute. You're telling me we have a potential infectious disease with a high mortality rate and a high infection rate. Are you sure it's contained?" I ask.

"Yes, yes. It is contained. No one comes out to this corner of Siberia unless you are a scientist or a tusker."

"But are you certain, Alexi?"

"Very," he says in a stern tone.

"Well, do we know where it came from? Has the genome been sequenced?" Dr. Fraser asks.

"No. Like I said earlier, no one has been to the camp."

"Well, what do we know?" I ask.

"We know that we have something with a high mortality rate and a high infection rate, but we don't know anything else," Alexi says.

Dr. Fraser and I are at our wits' ends. We now realize that we have to trace the pathogen's etiology, starting from the ground up.

CHAPTER 4:

THE CAMP

"Well, doctors, we have arrived," says Alexi.

"Where is it? Is there supposed to be some sort of grand entrance?" I inquire.

When I exit the SUV, I do a full 360 and see the same thing: trees. Lots of trees, and the trees don't even have leaves. Most of them have fallen to the ground, creating a goopy mess of mud and filth. I guess this is my "Welcome to Russia" moment. Looking at the untamed wilderness, I now realize that wearing Crocs was a very bad idea, but that's life: we live and learn.

On a side note, there's barely any snow on the ground, so I guess Alexi was right: the permafrost is thawing.

"That's the thing, Dr. Lawrence. We cannot set up camp in the epicenter. There's a higher risk of infection there. Therefore, we must establish a perimeter a couple of miles out. It's okay though because the terrain is relatively flat, so it shouldn't be a problem getting there in the coming days."

I shrug my shoulders and turn to Dr. Fraser. "So, uh, what do we do now?"

With her hands on her hips, she says, "I guess we need to set up a functioning camp, and then we'll formulate a plan."

"Alexi, my man. Is it just us? Like only the three of us? Because I have a feeling that setting up a camp isn't going to be easy with just the three of us."

"It's okay. I'm a very strong man."

"I don't doubt that, Alexi, but I think it would be better, for the less physically gifted, if we had help."

"No help. We can do it all on our own. The Russian government believes that we need to minimize contact in the infected region, so only the three of us for now."

Alexi leads the way, leaving faint footprints in the soft mud.

The SUV's trunk swings wide open and we start unloading the unwieldy wood crates and suitcases.

Like a well-organized military unit, we expertly unload the crates without a hiccup, until . . .

"Jesus. Dr. Fraser, did you have to pack everything and the kitchen sink? Alexi, how much does this weigh?"

"I'd say at least thirty-five kilograms."

"Uh. Rebecca, what's the conversion? I don't speak the metric system."

"First off, you are a physician, so you should use the metric system, and I'd say that it's about seventy pounds. Second, I think it's a reasonable amount to pack for an extended voyage. You know, Dr. Lawrence. Your bag is pretty heavy too. What are you hiding in there?" says Dr. Fraser.

"*Nothing*! There's nothing special in there. My bag is pretty capacious, so I figured, why not fill it to the brink? Am I right?"

My secret stash of barbecue sauce is safe for now.

"Well, okay then. Keep your little secrets to yourself," says Dr. Fraser.

After several hours, we finally finish unpacking and unloading the crates.

Base camp is almost complete. Almost.

All we have to do is construct a fully functioning tent. Keep in mind that I'm a physician who dabbles in infectious diseases, not an engineer nor an architect.

I've only had to build a tent once before. I was in northern Africa volunteering with the CDC's Epidemic Intelligence Service. We were tracking a chikungunya outbreak in Chad, and we formed our camp near the outskirts of a tiny, remote village. I, apparently, did not inspect my tent properly: the tent was festooned with holes, big ones too. How did the holes get there? I still don't know. All I know is that a very big, poisonous snake snuck inside and gave me a metaphorical heart attack when I woke up in the morning. I, fortunately, didn't get bit, but needless to say, after that whole debacle, I never worked with the Epidemic Intelligence Service again. However, I learned a lot about containing outbreaks and camping, which is great, but this is Siberia, not the Saharan country of Chad. The situation is more complex.

Luckily, Alexi is, well, the man. He deftly puts together all of the intricate little pieces, and *voilà!* We have a tent, sans struggle. It may not be the most luxurious of abodes, but it'll do.

A thick layer of grey clouds starts to form over us, blocking much of the light.

"Alexi, how many tents do we have?" says Dr. Fraser.

"Well, right now, we only have two, which means that somebody has to bunk."

Like children, Dr. Fraser and I yell, "Not it!" at the same time.

Sadly, I am a gentleman, and after much discussion, I decide that I must always let the lone lady bunk by herself.

"Alrighty then. Alexi, my man, it looks like tent number two is for the boys. We're going to have so much fun without Dr. Fraser pestering us."

"You know that I'm still here, right?" says Dr. Fraser.

Alexi and I shrug her off and continue setting up. The canvas and nylon tent are slowly starting to find its form amongst the inhospitable landscape. The once-untamed wilderness is starting to look like a legitimate campsite. There are three tents, two of which have been dedicated to a sleeping quarters, and the other is a multipurpose meeting room with a super low-tech white board. We spared no expense.

Although the tents are quite "spacious"—maybe eight by ten feet—it's quite cozy.

Before we know it, the sun sets and the clouds continue to block any residual light, leaving us with no choice but to call it quits for the day.

In order to protect us from any unwelcome and potentially dangerous animals, Alexi had me gather firewood from the surrounding area: logs, twigs, fallen branches, and the like. However, nearly everything was dank; the snowmelt seeped through any fallen branches, creating a moist environment, which is *no bueno* for a fire.

However, after much tribulation, Alexi, being the man that he is, eventually creates a fire out of thin air, like a true god of the north. Although he may have used copious amounts of vodka and several matches, I'm not complaining.

The snap and crackle of the fire complement the incessant heat radiating from the pit.

Sitting around the fire with a warm, yellow glow around his face, Alexi starts asking questions.

"So, doctors. Why did you get into the whole field of infectious diseases?"

"World domination," I reply.

Alexi laughs and tells me, "I've heard that one before."

I'm not sure what he means by that, but I continue entertaining him.

"You see, Alexi, I treat and diagnose all forms of infectious diseases in humans, but my favorite has to be viruses. Viruses are perhaps God's greatest and worst creation—if you believe in that, of course. They don't pick favorites. They can destroy entire civilizations, yet spare others. They infect almost every living thing on the planet. Nothing is safe. Not even humans, the smartest and most technologically advanced creature on the planet. In every other aspect of life, we reign supreme, yet when it comes to these microscopic things, we are nothing," I say.

Alexi leans closer to the fire, holding his hands inches from the rising flames.

"They practically use us, and when they're done hijacking our body's ingenious replication system, they can potentially kill us. That's where we come in. Without microbiologists like Dr. Fraser, we wouldn't know anything about these infectious agents, and without physicians like me, we wouldn't be able to properly treat infected individuals. We form a unique dynamic duo: she collects the samples and analyzes the data, and I apply the data and treat infected patients. Without us, these infectious agents would wreak havoc on society, culling millions of people. We try to locate these pesky pestilences before they have a chance to spread. However, it doesn't always work out. . . ." I start to reminisce on my time working in sub-Saharan Africa.

Dr. Fraser and Alexi are both stunned by my emotionally moving monologue. I guess I should've been an actor or a world leader.

"Wow. I've never thought of it that way. My line of work is not nearly as enjoyable, but it pays the bills," Alexi says.

Alexi's vagueness squashes any sentimental emotions that I may have been fostering from the previous monologue, and I inquire, "What would that be? If you don't mind me asking."

"Oh, boy. I did a lot of things. When I was a young boy, about eighteen or so, I always wanted to be in the military. It was the thing to do in the small town where I grew up. To leave the town, you had to join the military. That was the only way out, so I did. Sure, I was young, and I left my parents, but I don't regret it. It taught me a lot of unique skills," he says.

Dr. Fraser chimes in, "What was your job in the military?"

"I did lots of stuff. Fixed things, working as a mechanic. Then, they needed another grunt for a platoon that was shipping out, so I volunteered. Biggest mistake of my life, and after I returned, I quit the military. I was twenty-five at the time, and twenty-five-year-olds shouldn't go through the stuff that I went through."

"So, what did you do between the military and now?" I ask.

"Ah, I worked as a PMC, a private military contractor, doing mostly VIP protection. They paid really well, and I wasn't shipped out to foreign places all that much. I'm still doing the PMC stuff like I'm doing with you guys, but, uh, I don't know how many years I have left of it. I'm forty-six now, and I have other things to do," he sighs. "I do, however, hope that we're not out here for too long researching this thing. I don't think I can spend too long away from my children, or wife for that matter. Do either of you have children?"

"Not really," Dr. Fraser says.

Alexi cracks a smile and says, "Come on, Dr. Fraser, you either have kids or you don't. You can't 'not really' have them. Hahaha," he laughs as he cracks a smile.

"Fine. I don't have kids, nor do I want them," she says.

"Why not? My kids are the love of my life. Without them, I am nothing. Being a parent is the most rewarding thing ever. Even after a long day of work, coming home to my kids puts a smile on my face. You're telling me you don't want them?"

"That is correct. I've done the calculations, and to raise a child until they are eighteen, it will cost north of five hundred thousand dollars. . . ."

"But Dr. Fraser, it's not about the money. It's about having someone you love and cherish. You can't tell me that you don't want that!"

Dr. Fraser just sits there in her neon green foldable lawn chair, struggling to find the right words. Alexi has stumped a brainiac. Not bad for a soldier boy.

"So, Lawrence, what about you? Do you have kids?"

"That's a 'no' from me, captain. My brother, on the other hand, has settled down and has a family, so I'm not missing too much. He's got two little rug rats: a six-year-old boy and a four-year-old girl." I hand my phone to Alexi.

"Oh my! They are adorable, but they are not yours. How come?"

"Um, I haven't found the time with work. You probably don't have this problem, Alexi, but there aren't many pickup lines that revolve around infectious diseases."

Dr. Fraser chimes in: "Are you a virus? 'Cause I want to replicate inside you."

"*Get out!*" I yell. "Not funny. Never funny. . . . Since when did you decide to usurp my comedic role?"

Meanwhile, Alexi starts bursting into tears, laughing like he's never heard a joke before. I guess it was a real knee slapper, to him at least.

With Alexi's energetic laugh subsiding, I reply, "Anyway, I just haven't had the time."

Dr. Fraser chimes in again. "That's sort of my situation too. When you're stuck in a lab trying to sequence the genomes of viruses and bacteria for ten to twelve hours a day, you don't really get to socialise with many people."

"Ah, the joys of saving the world," I say.

An ominous silence envelops the campsite, and we just stare at the incessant flames of the fire—nature's television.

There we are. Three amigos just sitting by the fire, eating bargain brand beans with a possible pandemic festering a mile and a half away.

"Rise and shine, doctors. Today is a beautiful day in Siberia, and we must not waste it. We have a very big day ahead of us. We need to finish setting up the campsite and your lab."

Well, Alexi's literally eye-opening speech can only mean one thing: I didn't get eaten by a bear last night; the fire must have worked.

In my opinion, day one was a real hoot. My man, Alexi, and I are bunking, so it's just like college again, minus the black mold and asbestos from the dorms, of course.

I just have to declare one thing: I already hate camping. Don't get me wrong. What we're doing here is important work, but a shower would really boost my morale. Also, I haven't coiffed my hair in two days, and I resemble the finest of Chia Pets.

"Mornin', Rebecca. How'd you sleep without your favorite stuffed animal?"

"For the record, I slept fine even with your obnoxious conversation and Alexi spoiling the serenity."

"I mean, what was I supposed to do? Alexi was regaling with stories from his past. He's a true Russian legend among these parts."

"I'm sure he is. By the way, you look like Albert Einstein with that hairdo," she replies.

"Well, look who finally got a funny bone. I guess I'm not the only comedian in Siberia anymore."

As we sit around the smoldering embers of the fire, we munch on our knockoff Frosted Flakes, which to my surprise aren't that bad. I'm more of a Cinnamon Toast Crunch kind of guy, but I can't complain.

I inquire with a mouth full of food: "So, Alexi, how soon until our camp is fully operational, meaning how soon until we can investigate ground zero?"

"It all depends on your motivation. It's just the three of us for now, so we may be able to finish camp today, but that's unlikely. Most likely tomorrow."

"We've already wasted enough time. The pathogen was discovered about a week ago. It could be anywhere right now," says Dr. Fraser.

"Impossible!" exclaims Alexi. "The Russian government has set up a perimeter around the campsite. Nobody has gone in or left the campsite in two weeks. The pestilence has not left the campsite. That is final."

"Alrighty then. So, Rebecca, since our ostensible bacteria-virus-prion-thing has clearly *not* left the campsite, how do we build a level four biosafety laboratory out in the middle of, well, this?"

"I'm going to be honest with you: I have no clue. Dr. Lancaster did include an instruction manual; however, I don't think it comes with detailed pictures, so we're going to have to wing it and see where it goes."

"Woah. Is Dr. Fraser becoming a Dr. Lawrence? Has she abandoned her uptight ways and adopted a loosey-goosey outlook on life?"

Alexi butts in, "Don't be afraid, doctors. Back in my hometown, I worked a construction job one summer to make some extra cash. I know a thing a two about building."

"You see that? That's why Alexi is the man."

"Doctors, what is a level four biosafety laboratory exactly? What should I be expecting to build?" asks Alexi.

"Why don't you take this one, Rebecca? You are, after all, the leader of this clandestine operation and the trained researcher."

"Sure. In the research field, biosafety is classified into four distinct categories, from one to four. Biosafety level one, or BSL-1, is for pathogens or microbes that do not usually pose a significant human health hazard. Think E. coli. A BSL-1 facility is pretty barebones: you can perform the experiments on an open table or desk with varying degrees of personal protective equipment, or PPE, required. The next level is a step up. In a BSL-2 facility, you're usually working with things that have the potential to cause harm. Think salmonella. In this level, things are a bit more locked down. For instance, PPE is usually required and there needs to be a decontamination system in place, along with an eyewash station and sink," she says.[9]

---

9 "Biosafety in Microbiological and Biomedical Laboratories," US Department of Health and Human Services, Date Last Modified December, 2009.

"The next level is where things get dangerous. BSL-3 is what most people think of when they think of biosafety. Researchers are usually required to get vaccinations, and they even have to wear respirators, which can filter out the pathogens. Additionally, increased protection such as a biosafety cabinet—BSC—which is a fancy box with a protective shield that protects the scientist from accidental contamination, will be used. Because these pathogens are transmissible through respiration, a negative pressure system, in which air only flows into the room, will be deployed. What's really interesting is that most BSL-3 facilities have airlocks, which prevent the pathogen from escaping. However, BSL-3 pales in comparison to a BSL-4 facility," says Dr. Fraser.[10]

I butt in: "It's the mack daddy of them all, Alexi."

"Yes, to use Dr. Lawrence's word, it's the mack daddy of them all. In a BSL-4 facility, the researchers are required to change out of their clothes because of the high risk of transmission. Additionally, you need to go through a shower, either chemical or regular, upon exiting. Finally, a BSL-4 facility is usually a separate entity, like a solid concrete box, to prevent the pathogen from unintentionally escaping. Now, there's two types of BSL-4 facilities. There's one where you need to don the proper PPE, a positive pressure suit that makes you look like an oompa loompa," says Dr. Fraser.

"Wait, I wouldn't say you look like an oompa loompa. I think you look more like that girl who turned into a blueberry. Alexi, do you remember that from the film? I can't remember her name."

---

10 "Laboratory Biosafety Manual: Third Edition," World Health Organization, Date Last Modified 2004.

Alexi raises his eyebrows in confusion. I guess he's never seen *Willy Wonka*. I'll have to fix that eventually.

"Sure. You look like the blueberry girl. Now, the positive pressure suit provides a constant stream of air, so that nothing can breach or enter your suit. In the case of an accidental leak, air flows out of the suit with the goal of blocking the pathogen from entering and infecting the scientist. With the proper suit, you can usually just work with a regular BSL-2 table. Although this may be the most common type of BSL-4 facility, the other type involves a class three biosafety cabinet and is pretty high tech. Without going into too much detail, it's basically a giant glass box that allows the researcher to manipulate the virus with gloves without directly touching it. Either way, the room needs to be a negative pressure system, and you'll have to get a shower afterwards," says Dr. Fraser.

Once again, I provide an interlude: "Since we're dealing with a pathogen of unknown origin, which may or may not be highly infectious and deadly, we need to take the utmost caution. Now, we don't really have time to fly samples back and forth between our lab because, well, we're out in BFE. As a result, the Russians and Australians have agreed we should construct an on-site lab in order to rapidly test the pathogen and diagnose the situation. That's where the BSL-4 lab comes into play. Because this thing—whether it's a virus, bacteria, or prion—is a bad boy, we need to transform that shipping container into a high-tech biosafety laboratory that meets the World Health Organization's international standards."

"I think we better get to work then," says Alexi.

∗ ∗ ∗

"Alright, what's the plan, o captain, my captain?"

"Well, in layman's speak, there's a forty-foot shipping container over there, and it has your name on it," says Dr. Fraser.

I'm jubilated. She wants me, me of all people, to have the honor of opening the shipping container.

Following orders, I casually walk over to the matte black container and try to pry open the two steel doors.

"Hey, Rebecca, there's a passcode."

"A what? Hold on, I'm coming."

"You see? There's a passcode. I tried my birthdate, but that isn't it."

"You really tried your birthdate?"

"Yeah, why not? Dr. Lancaster and I are solid friends. I thought: *maybe . . .*"

"I'm surprised you didn't try one-two-three-four."

"That was the first thing I tried," I laugh.

I continue to tinker with the lock for several minutes while Dr. Fraser searches her purse for a manilla envelope.

"Ah! Ok, here it is. Try one-zero-one-two."

Lo and behold, it works.

Upon opening the sturdy doors, we are immediately taken aback by how immaculate everything looks.

The outside of the container is rather drab. It's painted in a midnight black with a lone plexiglass windowpane on one side. However, on the inside, everything is neat and white, with several shop lights dangling from the ceiling. Everything is neatly placed into boxes and stacked in a Tetris-like fashion.

"Here it is, Lawrence. This big box here is our class three biosafety cabinet, so I guess we're abiding by the cabinet laboratory standards now."

"Ah, man. I kind of wanted to wobble around in a puffed-up blue suit. Oh well, maybe next time."

"Give me a hand with it, please," says Dr. Fraser.

As we start to delicately unpack our shipping container full of goodies, Alexi patiently stands there outside, regarding the wilderness.

Dr. Fraser then turns to me and says, "By the way, since Alexi isn't in here, there's no way this thing is contained. There were no checkpoints, I haven't seen any routine military patrols, and Alexi's tone wasn't very frank."

"Yeah. I'm starting to doubt what really happened here. I guess we'll have to wait and see for ourselves."

"I guess so."

When all of the boxes are unpacked, Dr. Fraser gives Alexi a briefing on the specifics.

"Alright, Alexi. Since there's only three of us, we're going to have some problems. Namely, the US Centers for Disease Control, or some other organisation like that, has created a set of rules that researchers must follow when they are conducting work on highly infectious diseases like this new one. For instance, it requires a buddy system when working inside the BSL-4 laboratory. As a result, Dr. Lawrence and I will be inside; however, we need you to be on the outside monitoring our communication and all of the other technical aspects like pressure and temperature. Can you do that?" Dr. Fraser asks.

"Yes, yes. I can handle that for now."

"Good. Dr. Lawrence will give you a rundown of the equipment while I go call Dr. Lancaster and tell him we've almost set up the lab."

"Alright, Alexi, my man. As you can tell, this monstrosity of a creation is our makeshift BSL-4 laboratory. Now, I'm sure that this may be breaking some international laws and what not, but hey, that's how progress is made."

"That is correct."

"Wonderful. So, you'll primarily be on the outside, right here. Now, from this window you should be able to see my handsome self and Dr. Fraser. Here is a touch screen monitor, which will allow you to monitor all the technical aspects like pressure, water level, temperature—all that jazz. Dr. Fraser will go over the specifics of the specifics with you because I honestly don't know much about it. I'm the physician of the group; I've only worked in a BSL-4 facility twice before, so I'm still learning as well."

Alexi vigorously nods his head in agreement.

"Now on the inside, we have our class three BSC. It's this big boxy looking thing. It's got windows all around, and the inside is free of any sharp or abrasive material. We can manipulate and experiment on the pathogen by using these four thick rubber gloves. These gloves basically allow us to safely work with the pathogen in an albeit limited mobility. Um, what else? Oh yeah, here is the autoclave system, which is basically a fancy dishwasher-slash-airlock, which allows us to bring samples in and out. Again, without going into the specifics, it basically uses high heat and steam to sort of sterilize the materials."

"What are those big hoses coming out the top of the machine?"

"Ah, yes. Those tubes bring in air from the outside and take contaminated air out of the box. The air that comes in goes through one HEPA air filter, and the air that leaves goes through two. At the end of it all, it's spick and span. Like

Rebecca said earlier, the whole box is under a negative pressure system, which yadda yadda yadda keeps the pathogen in. You get the point."

"Yes, I do. It's a little complicated, but I can manage it."

"Over there. That's all of our lab equipment, like PCR machines. We'll discuss that later, but for now, we need to finish setting up our lab and begin running diagnostics."

When Alexi and I finish our conversation, Dr. Fraser conveniently returns.

"What's up, doc? What did my overlord have to say?"

"Nothing much. He asked how we were handling things. I gave him a synopsis of what we've done so far, and I told him he made a wise choice in choosing me as the leader."

"Ouch. Did he ask how I was doing?"

"Surprisingly, he did. He wanted to know how the Crocs were holding up."

"Classic Dr. Lancaster. What else did he say?"

"He said the heads of state for some major countries, like the United States, Australia, and others, got together to discuss the ongoing situation. Apparently, we're an international team now, whatever that means. Also, he wants us to have boots on the ground by tomorrow at 1400 hours. Now, that mandate was at the request of, not Dr. Lancaster, but the Australian prime minister, so we can't miss that deadline."

"Alrighty then. I've briefed Alexi on the basics, and I've started to run diagnostics on our equipment. I do see one potential problem: we only have so much petrol. I'm not sure how long it's going to last with the generator going twenty-four seven."

"We'll have to worry about that at some point, but for now we have enough to last us a week. We can always have Alexi phone a friend if need be," says Dr. Fraser.

"Alright. The diagnostic results should come in soon. Unfortunately, we've squandered most of the day setting up our mobile lab, so it looks like our dance with death will have to be tomorrow."

"It looks that way, Lawrence."

CHAPTER 5:

EPICENTER

"You ready, Rebecca?"

"Not yet. Dr. Lancaster just sent us the revised predict protocols, so we're going to have to adjust our plans."

"In what way?"

"Well, the new protocols complicate things."

"Ain't that lovely?"

Alexi calmly struts into the makeshift meeting room with an upbeat mentality.

"What's up, doctors? So, today is the big day. Huh?"

Alexi reaches over the cheap plastic table, and we perform our secret handshake in front of a mystified Dr. Fraser.

With a tilt of the head, Dr. Fraser says, "What? What was that?"

"Nothing. Just a bit of fun. Fun never hurt anybody. You should try it sometime," I reply

"I bet it does," Dr Fraser says.

Alexi takes the only open seat across the table, and Dr. Fraser commences the meeting.

"As you two may know, we are about to enter into an exclusion zone set up by the Russian government in order to limit the spread of this highly infectious pathogen. Now, because of the strict protocols we must follow, I am obliged to give you a certain set of concrete rules that you must follow at all times. No exceptions."

"Well, don't keep us waiting, Rebecca. Let's get this show on the road."

"Alright, here are the rules. First, because this is a pathogen of unknown origin, it may be highly infectious with a very high mortality rate, or it may not. We don't know yet. As a result, if you would like to back out, now would be the time to say so. Are both of you okay with this expedition?"

Alexi and I both shake our noggins and give an audible "yes."

"Good. Just a couple more house rules. Second, you are required to wash your hands pretty much at any given time. I know, I know. Soap and water will be hard to come by in the epicentre, so each of you will be given a bottle of hand sanitiser, which is, by mandate, sixty percent alcohol. Next, please, for love of God, don't wear your personal clothes to the epicentre. This one is mostly for you, Lawrence. I don't want you wandering around in Crocs or that stupid graphic tee you constantly wear."

"What? My Metallica T-shirt? Alexi, help me out here."

"I think it's a great shirt. Very good music," says Alexi.

"It's arcane," she says, holding back a barrage of potentially negative comments. "Look," she exhales, "just put on the disposable scrubs and we'll all be fine. The main point is simple: don't do anything stupid, and don't bring this thing back to camp. If we follow those rules, we should make it out okay."

"Um, 'should' is not very reassuring. I mean, look at Alexi. The fear in his eyes is palpable."

Alexi, the mysterious man of the mountains of Russia, is sitting in a foldable chair and popping almonds into his mouth like they are Skittles. Upon noticing we are talking about him, he stops and gives us one of those halfhearted smiles.

"Very great!" he says as he gives us a thumbs up.

"Allow me to adjust my phraseology for the hoi polloi," she says. "If you wear the proper personal protective equipment—PPE—you will come back safe with no infections. Capisce?"

"Yeah, yeah. Capisce. Um. So, what type of PPE are we going to wear for this oh-so-routine field expedition? I don't want it to clash with my Crocs," I say as I crack a smile.

"Not funny, Lawrence."

"It kind of was, but we digress. Continue," I reply.

"There's a whole list of factors we need to consider before we make a decision. Here's my general thinking as of right now: In our special case, we're going to work with a dead mammoth, so the risk of bites, scratches, or any other anomaly resulting from handling live animals is very low, which is good. However, that's about the only good part. Unfortunately, because of this pathogen's reported infectivity, we have to take the utmost caution. There are numerous potential exposure opportunities and routes of infection. There will be open needles, potentially sharp rocks or sticks, and other bad things to watch out for. This pathogen could be transmissible by blood or other bodily fluids, or it could be transmitted through another means. We just don't know, so we have to prepare for everything."

"Right on. Do we know what risk factor the World Health Organization classified this outbreak as, assuming that they have been given any information on it?"

"No, Dr. Lancaster didn't tell me anything about that yet. In my honest opinion, with what I know, it's most likely going to be in risk group three or four."

"I'm sorry, Dr. Fraser. What do the risk groups mean?" asks an inquisitive Alexi.

"I can take this one, Rebecca. I've been researching."

"Oh, have you? I didn't know that you could read."

"You've used that joke before, and yes, I can. Quite well, actually," I respond. "Now, Alexi, the World Health Organization (WHO) has created some nifty categories that we scientists can use to classify an outbreak. In the WHO risk group one, we're usually dealing with a pathogen that is unlikely to be a human health hazard and thus poses little or no risk. Next, we have the risk group two. In this group, we have a pathogen that can cause harm in humans but poses little risk to researchers and the community because of available treatment options. In the third risk group, things get dicey. These pathogens pose a serious risk to the researcher, but they are unlikely to spread from one individual to another. Finally, we have the WHO risk group four, which deals with pathogens that are highly infectious and can be transmitted from one individual to another. Oh, and there's also not normally a vaccine for risk group four pathogens. It's peculiarly similar to the biosafety classifications. How'd I do, Rebecca?"[11]

"It seems like a rendition that was influenced by Wikipedia, but it'll do right now."

With that, the meeting ends and we clear off the papers that were strewn across the table.

Like baby ducks with their mother, we follow Dr. Fraser outside of the tent to an unmarked wooden crate outside of our makeshift BSL-4 facility.

"To answer your earlier question, Lawrence, this is our PPE," she says as she opens up the crate. "This area outside

---

11   "Laboratory Biosafety Manual," 1-3.

of the shipping container is where we'll suit up with our PPE, and when we're about to return from our expedition at the campsite, we'll remove our PPE before we get into the SUV to minimise the risk of spreading the virus. Alright, so let's get onto the specifics. For the main outer covering, we are going to be wearing a Tychem coverall. It's this white one-sie-looking thing here."

It's a much nicer day than yesterday. It reminds me of southern California, no clouds in the light blue sky. A lot of the excess water froze over last night, so it's less muddy as well, which is better for us because it means there's less of a chance of slipping. It still fells eerie out here. There's nobody for miles and miles. In fact, I think that . . .

"What are you doing, Lawrence?"

"Daydreaming."

"Well, stop," she sternly demands. "Anyway, these coveralls will protect you from possible contamination. In our case, it will most likely be blood or fluid samples that we collect. They're also less prone to tears and rips; however, they're only *less* prone. They're not invincible, so please don't go roughhousing in them. They're delicate like a baby. The protocol also recommends that we wear plastic aprons, but I don't think I'm going to torture you two with that."

"Rebecca, we're going to look like marshmallows wearing this. Did you have to get the all-white Tychem coveralls? I'm pretty sure I saw one in a movie once that was orange and made out of a more durable material. I'm just saying. Fashion never hurt anybody."

"I will not acknowledge any snide remarks," she says. "Next, we have the reusable, rubber boots. We're going to have to disinfect them with a chlorine footbath before we leave the epicentre so we don't carry the pathogen back to camp. However, they should provide a nice protection for our feet: we don't know if there are any sharp items lying around in the camp. Once again, Lawrence, no Crocs."

"Understood. Crocs are a no go on this one. Maybe next time."

"Now, Dr. Lancaster was kind enough to give us a choice for our respiration system. Alexi, since you're going to stay with the SUV while we collect samples, we're going to have you wear an N95 mask with goggles. On the other hand, since Dr. Lawrence and I are going into the hot zone, we will be wearing a powered air-purifying respirator, or a PAPR system. The N95 masks are great, but the PAPR system is reusable, and it's a battery-powered system that pumps air to a full-face mask. Either way, we're going to be protected against any aerosolised pathogens."

"What about the gloves, Rebecca? How could you forget about the gloves?"

"I didn't forget. I was saving the most important part of our attire for the end. Now, as Dr. Lawrence eloquently pointed out, we're going to be wearing gloves, specifically nitrile gloves. We're using nitrile gloves because they are most resistant to breakage as opposed to latex gloves. However, we're going to be wearing two pairs of gloves since we're going to be using sharps, such as needles, when we draw blood.

"Finally, when we're done with our mission, we're going to be disposing our equipment in these bright red biohazard bags," says Dr. Fraser. "Any questions?"

Like scared students during an English class discussion on a Friday afternoon, Alexi and I stand there without saying a word.

"Alright, we leave in thirty minutes then," she replies.

✳ ✳ ✳

Sitting in the front seat of the dilapidated SUV, I stare out through the partially cracked windshield admiring the picturesque scenery for, potentially, the last time. It's really quite breathtaking. The light brown soil is blanketed with a thin layer of melting snow, and the sparsely packed trees create a natural mix of game trails and pathways.

While I sit there regarding God's creation, the car door behind me slams shut.

"Jesus, man. Can you knock? Rebecca, you almost gave me a heart attack."

"Are you ready for this?" says Dr. Fraser.

"I'm never ready for anything. Also, you look cute in that PPE, like a human-sized marshmallow."

"Yeah, yeah, yeah. Very funny," she says in a snarky tone. "Here's the final plan. You and I are going to go investigate the reported crime scene and take some samples. I'd rather take more than enough because, well, I don't want to make two trips. Do you understand?"

"Yes, I do. Trust me, I don't want to dance with the devil either."

Through the windows, we can see Alexi making a beeline for our car.

"My god. He's waddling like a penguin. Look, Rebecca."

"Enough, David Attenborough. Focus on the task at hand."

"That's easy for you to say. I have stuff to live for."

"Really? Like what?"

"Well, I have . . ."

The car door opens, and Alexi finally makes his way into the driver's seat of the SUV.

"Okay, are you ready, doctors? We go."

"I guess you'll never know, Rebecca."

"Know what?" Alexi says.

"Doesn't matter, Alexi. All that matters is you stay with the car while Dr. Lawrence and I go out and collect samples. We rationalise that two people in the exclusion zone are more than enough," Dr. Fraser says.

"That's okay with me. I don't want to be in there either," says Alexi.

"One important thing I only briefly mention is the decontamination process. When we're finished with our scientific endeavours, we're going to need to decontaminate ourselves. At the end, we'll do this by giving ourselves a chemical shower with what is effectively bleach. Everything disposable that we're wearing will be thrown away into the red biohazard bags, which will be burned when we get back to camp. For the boots and our hoods, we're going to decontaminate those with pure bleach before we leave as well. That should destroy any viral particles," says Dr. Fraser.

"Doctors, you never told me this mask was going to be uncomfortable."

"Yeah, I know, Alexi. Ain't that the truth, my man."

* * *

Within no time, the car stops, and Alexi makes a declaration.

"We have arrived. I've parked about a half mile away from the mining camp, so that should give us a nice buffer."

We nervously unpack our backpacks and other equipment from the car, and with a slam of the trunk, we are off, walking south toward the campsite.

With Alexi behind us, we start discussing each other's roles as we gracefully glide over rocks and other fallen debris.

"Alright, so Lawrence, I'll handle most of the sampling, because, frankly, I don't trust you with sharps."

"I'm fine with that. Less chance of me accidentally infecting myself."

"You will, however, need to hold the cooler though," she says.

"Wait, why do I have to hold cooler full of potentially infected mammoth parts?"

"Because it's the most important job. Without those samples, research would stall, and this thing could become a pandemic. If anything, you're the MVP here."

"If I'm the Tom Brady of the team, I'll do it."

We walk for about another five minutes, trembling over fallen branches and sliding in the slick mud. My white suit has turned slightly brown from the mud.

Then we finally see it. The campsite.

It's a wasteland that's perched near a cascade and a small but navigable river. There is garbage everywhere. Crushed beer cans, vodka bottles, and plastic bags pepper the location like a fraternity house on a Monday morning. What remains of the snow (that hasn't melted) is covered in a thick layer of fresh mud. It has a Chernobyl feel to it. Nothing has been touched in about two weeks. The tents are still ripped open, presumably by fallen branches; sleeping bags are still strewn about in an awkward fashion; and the massive water pumps are still turned on yet have run out of gasoline.

All of this means they left in a hurry.

"Would you look at this place, Rebecca? It's dirtier than my freshman dorm. Jeez."

"I know. I guess let's check what's left of the tents first. Remember, try not to touch anything that looks ominous."

"I don't know what an 'ominous' thing would look like. Precision of language, Rebecca."

"If it looks yucky or something like that, don't touch it," she says as she smiles in through her clear face shield.

One by one, we check each tent, rummaging through anything that isn't "yucky looking." However, our efforts prove fruitless as we find nothing of interest. There's just trash, and lots of it.

"Isn't it interesting how we haven't found any bodies yet?" says Dr. Fraser.

"I guess so. The tuskers may have scampered off. Maybe they saw what this thing was doing, and they hightailed it out of here. I doubt they made it very far though. Most of their gasoline is used to power their water pumps, so I can't see them wasting it on a spontaneous journey to get a Twix bar. Something must've happened," I say.

"You're probably right."

"Or, hear me out on this one. The Russian military could've come in and cleared the place out before we could investigate."

"As far-fetched as that sounds, it's a possibility—albeit an unlikely one," she says. "I want to know why the Russians would've taken the bodies."

"Looks like we have another Dyatlov Pass Incident on our hands," I reply.

She neglects to respond to my comment, presumably because she is uneducated in Siberian folklore. She should hang out with Alexi more often.

"Do you see any cars?" she says.

"No, but look at this. It looks like a tire tread. Looks like it's been here for a couple of days at least, maybe a week or two."

"Interesting. Either they left on their own volition, or we may not be the first people on the campsite after all. Let's keep looking," says Dr. Fraser

After meandering around for a while longer, we eventually discover the entrance to a gargantuan cave tucked away in the mountainside.

"Should we go in, Lawrence?"

"As much as I'd love to say I've explored a cave in the Siberian tundra, I think I'm going to have to pass on this one."

"I'm the leader, so follow me," says Dr. Fraser.

"Why did I have to pick this job? Why couldn't I have joined the Navy or worked on Wall Street like all my friends?"

As we enter into the cave the light begins to fade, and we become entombed in darkness.

"Turn on your flashlight, Lawrence."

"Copy that." I unsheathe my military-grade, titanium black flashlight, which I got at a garage sale.

Under the slim beam of the LED light, we meander through the cramped corridor. On either side, jagged rocks protrude like a scene out of Indiana Jones.

Dr. Fraser leads the way, leaving me in the back with the awkward Styrofoam cooler.

Without her aide, I constantly rub my suit against the abrasive and jagged rocks, which, unbeknownst to me, produces a small hairline tear in the side of my not-so-invincible Tychem suit.

However, I never notice, and when we reach the end of the corridor, we discover a treasure trove of white gold.

"Is that, um. Is that a . . ."

"A woolly mammoth?" says Dr. Fraser.

"Yeah. That's the word."

The cavern widens into a fifteen- by twenty-five foot clearing, revealing two, maybe three, woolly mammoths stuck in the mud and the thawing permafrost. Under the incessant beam of our faint LED flashlights, the stalactites glow, casting a unique light pattern onto the exposed torso of the mammoth carcasses.

"Here, look at this one. It looks like a young adult, and then this gushy-looking thing over there looks like the matriarch of the group," Dr. Fraser says jubilantly.

"The young adult still looks in good shape. It still has some nappy and matted fur. Granted it has seen better days, but still. "

Now, let me be clear. It does not look like an ordinary mammoth with all the fluffy fur and the big long tusks. Rather, it looks like roadkill that's been left on the side of a highway for several days. There are no maggots or anything like that, but the mammoth now has an oblong shape, which it most definitely didn't have before. The mammoth's once-lush hair looks all matted and its tusks are no longer present, presumably taken by the tuskers. She's a goopy one at that.

"Didn't Alexi say something about the permafrost acting like a meat locker?"

"Yes, he did," I reply.

Following protocol, we immediately unpack our equipment—needles, syringes, and the like.

"Wait, before we start dissecting this behemoth, get a quick picture of me with it. This will kill it with the ladies back home."

"I'm not going to do that," says Dr. Fraser.

"Fine, just take the picture for Dr. Lancaster then. I bet he's worried about us."

"Alright, I'm doing it only because it's for Dr. Lancaster."

As Dr. Fraser shows me the screen, I say, "That is perhaps the greatest screensaver of all time."

Now that the fun is over, we begin our work.

Following protocol, Dr. Fraser uses a clean scalpel to ablate what remains of the mammoth's outer skin and hair.

"So, Rebecca. What type of samples do we need to get again?"

"Well, first and foremost, we need to get a blood sample. Then, if we can, I'd like to obtain a spit sample, but that'll be unlikely, considering I can't identify its anterior or posterior ends. Additionally, I'd love to get a spleen and liver sample if we can. Remember, I don't want to make two trips."

As we begin peeling back the layers of skin, we realize that this specimen is incredibly well preserved.

"Woah, look Rebecca, the muscle tissues look like a red steak. I mean, light me a grill, I'm back with the boys."

With condescending eyes, Dr. Fraser says, "I know. I guess this specimen was preserved in pure ice rather than just permafrost, which may explain the abnormal preservation quality. I guess this poor creature fell into a lake and maybe drowned?"

"I'll take your word for it. I'm not a paleontologist."

Using an ice pick, we slowly chip away ice away from the underside of the mammoth, exposing its hind leg and a large portion of its stomach.

"Oh shit, oh shit, Lawrence I need your help!"

"What did you do, Rebecca?"

"I guess I punctured a vein because blood is flowing out. Hurry—get a syringe and a specimen bag."[12]

---

12   Katie Wong, "Can a Mammoth Carcass Really Preserve Flowing Blood and Possibly Live Cells?" *Nature,* May 30, 2013.

"Here, here. Don't cry over spilled milk. Or should I say spilled blood?"

"Not the time, Lawrence. Help me hold the skin back."

So, I sit there, holding back a gelatinous flap of mammoth skin, while Dr. Fraser sticks a needle into a mammoth's artery.

"Alright, that wasn't too bad. I've always wanted to look like a human Jackson Pollack painting, and good thing I didn't wear the ol' Crocs today. Huh?"

Dr. Fraser just sits in the mud with sweat beads and mammoth blood dripping down her face. I should also point out that I am in no better position: I have blood all over my Tychem suit, covering my posterior (chest) and anterior (back).

"Yeah. I guess so. These samples should be enough for genetic testing."

"Wait, Rebecca, how is this creature's blood still flowing? Shouldn't the blood be frozen?"

"I have no clue. It could have some sort of cold-weather protection built in, sort of like an antifreeze solution in cars. Some animals, like arctic ground squirrels, have some sort of cryoprotectant, which protects them from below freezing temperatures, but it's never been scientifically proven. For instance, arctic species are known to have haemoglobin that is insensitive to temperature changes, meaning it is more tolerant of colder temperatures. This would allow the woolly mammoth to oxygenate tissues below zero temperatures, which is something that most mammals cannot do.[13]

---

13   Jodie L. Rummer, "How Woolly Mammoth Blood Cheated the Cold," *Journal of Experimental Biology* 213, no. 15 (August 2010).

"However, a much more likely explanation is that the blood is flowing because it's contaminated. Water from the melting permafrost may have seeped inside the mammoth and, more or less, reenergized what was left in the mammoth's blood, allowing it to flow. Once we get back to the lab, we need to test to see whether or not this is actually blood and is not just water from their hoses or ice mixed with muscle tissue."[14]

"Very, very interesting," I reply.

"Also, don't get too excited just yet because we still need to get a spit sample and a liver sample."

"Alright, now which end is its head?"

After some time, we manage to get all the samples that we deem essential. Shockingly, we had no troubles obtaining a spit sample. Weird, I know.

As quick as we came, we start to pack up and hightail it out of the spooky, scary cave.

"Lawrence, put these samples in the cooler."

"Why do we need a cooler when it's literally freezing outside? Don't you think that it kind of defeats the purpose?"

"Here we go again. For starters, it's protocol. Second, as soon as the samples are removed from their subzero environment, they start to decay. Their genetic material practically disintegrates. By storing the samples in liquid nitrogen at around −196 degrees Celsius, we can prolong the lifespan of any viral particles and mammoth DNA."

---

14   Anna Liesowska, "Exclusive: The First Pictures of Blood From a 10,000-Year-Old Siberian Woolly Mammoth," *The Siberian Times*, May 29, 2013.

"Fair enough. I really am the MVP of this whole operation."

"If that makes you feel better while you stand there holding a box of decaying mammoth blood, then yes."

We begin the arduous journey of transporting the twenty-kilogram cooler back to Alexi's SUV.

Out of nowhere, a prominent gust of wind causes a rogue branch to snap off from the Siberian larch tree. The branch narrowly misses my shoulder; however, it knocks me, and the all-important cooler, off my balance, causing me to slip on the dank mud.

"Whoa!"

Lucky for me, Dr. Fraser, being the sweetheart that she is, manages to catch the cooler (but not me).

"You okay there, bud?" asks Dr. Fraser.

Covered in mud and looking like a soiled pig, I reply, "Never better."

"Lucky for you, the car is just over there."

Alexi sees us and starts waving, like a child waving to his incredibly handsome father.

"Oh boy, Alexi. You missed some crazy stuff, my man. First, I had to fight off several attackers, and then I had to single handedly carry about one hundred and fifty pounds of equipment back from the battlefield. I'm a true war hero."

"I do not believe anything you say, Dr. Lawrence."

"Ah, worth a shot at least."

"Alright, we now need to disinfect ourselves and the cooler."

I'll spare you the nitty-gritty of me taking a chemical shower. You probably don't need the visualization.

∗ ∗ ∗

After our ablutions we load up the rest of our equipment in the SUV and hightail it out of there.

"So, doctors. How was it besides all of the attackers and what not?"

"Back to Alexi's question, so it was . . ."

Dr. Fraser cuts me off, "I'll take this one, Lawrence. Alexi, it was bizarrely eerie. The place hadn't been touched for weeks. There were no bodies, nothing. There were just tents and equipment lying around."

I guess she doesn't want me spouting my unfounded conspiracy theories. What a true scientist.

"Very interesting. Like I said, no one has visited the camp since we learned about it. The bodies probably decayed."

I don't buy Alexi's "they decayed" argument. Here's the deal: For a body to decay, it needs heat and some form of detritivore to decompose the body. In the northern regions, especially in the Arctic Circle, they don't have either of these things. Alexi should know that, since he is a native Russian, so I still think something fishy happened here.

"Also, the mammoths were incredibly well preserved. When we dissected one, it still had organs, and blood even flowed out through one of the veins."

"It is entirely possible. I once heard a story about a man who discovered a mammoth calf in the Yamal Peninsula up near the Arctic. This calf was named Lyuba, and she was forty-one thousand years old. However, she was pristine; there was fur on her body, and she even had organs. I remember hearing about a scientist who was able to identify her diet based on the contents of her stomach. It's crazy, but that's the permafrost for you. It traps away Russia's past, no matter how deadly or innocent. Did you guys find everything okay?"[15]

"Yes, we did. We managed to sample blood from one mammoth, which should give us a good indication of whether or not a virus or bacteria has decided to highjack the mammoth's body. If there is a pathogen located somewhere in the sample, we should be able to isolate it and figure out its genetic sequence."

"Very nice. What about you, Dr. Lawrence?"

"I'm wet, cold, and there's a lot of cool liquid running down my back right now."

"Ah, yes. Sweating like a real man, Lawrence. That's what Russia does to you! The good thing is we're back at the base camp. You can relax and take a shower now."

As we exit the vehicle and unload our supplies, we notice someone standing outside of our BSL-4 staring in our general direction.

Intrigued, I ask, "Hey, bud, who are you?"

---

15   Tom Mueller, "Ice Baby," *National Geographic*, May 2009.

CHAPTER 6

THE HOT ZONE

"Allow me to introduce myself. My name is Igor Popov, and I will be your scientific liaison who will assist you in your experiments."

Dr. Fraser and I stand there dumbfounded.

Igor is a frail man, maybe in his late fifties, with salt-and-pepper-colored hair. His wire-rimmed glasses are straight out of the 1950s, but I don't think he cares too much about fashion.

"Hello, Igor. I'm Dr. Fraser, the head of this operation, and this is my partner . . ."

She nudges my right arm, forcing me to speak.

"Um. Hi, Igor. I'm Dr. Lawrence. I don't mean to be blunt like a good ol' rusty fishing knife, but, uh, what does being a scientific liaison entail?"

"Well, I am one of the head scientists at the State Research Center of Virology and Biotechnology, otherwise known as the Vector Institute, in Novosibirsk. The Kremlin informed me that you may be in need of assistance."

"What type of assistance did they mention?" inquires Dr. Fraser.

"They said you may need help operating the BSL-4 facility. They alerted me that you are in need of an exterior operator who can control the communication and pressure systems."

"I'll need to go talk with Dr. Lancaster to see what he says about this, so Dr. Lawrence, you're in charge while I'm gone," says Dr. Fraser.

Dr. Fraser trudges away, leaving a trail of faint imprints in the mud.

With the sound of the mud squishing and squashing echoing throughout the camp, Alexi and Igor start pleading their case.

"Dr. Lawrence, Igor is a very good researcher. I can assure you of that," says Alexi.

"I don't doubt that. You look like a splendid guy, Igor," I say as I wave in Igor's direction. "However, what happened to your government's plan of 'limiting exposure' in the epicenter? Doesn't this seem counterintuitive to bring in another member? No offense, Dr. Popov."

"You see, Dr. Lawrence, I am not very comfortable running a BSL-4 facility. I am just a chauffeur. Dr. Popov, on the other hand, is a trained scientist who works with BSL-4 facilities regularly. He is much better for the job."

"Allow me to add to that, Dr. Lawrence," Igor says. "Yes, I was sent on behalf of the Russian government in order to assess the situation. However, let me be clear: I am only here to assess the situation and will only help out when required. I have been instructed by my superiors to follow any instructions given by your team. We are not here to delay anything, only to assist when needed."

I stand there, shrugging my shoulders, and I say, "I don't know, chief. I'll go check in with the boss and see what she thinks."

"Please, go," says Alexi.

* * *

"Rebecca, what did Dr. Lancaster say?"

"Well, for starters, he thinks this is a very bad idea allowing Igor to run the BSL-4 facility. He said that neither the AID team nor the WHO were alerted that there would be a fourth member, so to them it's very suspicious."

"Yeah, tell me about it. The nearest town is several hours away by car, so I don't think this was a spontaneous trip. Not to mention, this Igor guy is suspicious. He's one of the head scientists of a BSL-4 in Novosibirsk, and they sent him out here. Really? Why would they send one of their chief scientists out into the field? The whole thing seems *tuna* fishy."

"Here's the bad news. Dr. Lancaster said that since we're guests in a Russian territory, we shouldn't offend them in any way. We don't want them to prematurely kick us out. We've gathered samples, but we still need to get them out of the country first. Because of this, he has mandated that we allow Igor to stay."

"Rebecca, I want to say this for the record. This is a very, very bad idea. We're allowing a complete stranger to operate our communication system and monitor our pressure systems. Imagine what will happen if there's a pressure leak or a biocontainment issue and he does nothing."

"Look, I know. However, orders are orders, and we have to follow them. Besides, Igor may know something that we don't."

"Yeah, he may know a lot more than he's telling us. I used to know a guy who looked like him, Rebecca. Do you know what happened?"

"What happened?" she inquires.

"Doesn't matter. He's in jail now. He did something to make some people angry, but that's besides the point. They both look alike."

"Lawrence, I think you've spent too much time watching movies."

"Alright, but I warned you. If the CIA asks me if anything was fishy, I'm going to cave."

"Please, just stop talking," she says

After our brief chinwag, we start walking back about ten meters or so.

Upon our return, Dr. Fraser breaks the good news to Igor Popov, aka Papa Igor.

"Alright, Dr. Popov, my superior, Dr. Lancaster of the AID, has informed me that you have been granted permission to join our team" says Dr. Fraser.

"That is fantastic news!" says Igor.

"Now, we're going to need to debrief you on what we've already done so you can be up to speed. Unfortunately, the night is rapidly approaching, so there will be no testing today," says Dr. Fraser.

"That is okay," says Igor.

As night rapidly approaches, we shuffle into the main tent erected in the center of the camp.

Sitting around the cheap plastic table, we debrief our new friend, Papa.

"So, Dr. Popov. For the past several days, we have been constructing and maintaining the camp, and today was the first day we actually entered into the exclusion zone. Alexi was told to wait by the SUV while Dr. Lawrence and I explored the mining site and collected samples. We discovered no bodies, only old tyre tracks in the mud. The tents were festooned with garbage—vodka bottles, beer cans, and so on," Dr. Fraser says.

"Looked like a college dorm, Dr. Popov," I interrupt.

"Or it looks like your tent, Dr. Lawrence, after just two days!" Alexi quips.

Alexi and Igor start chuckling while Dr. Fraser and I just sit there in silence. I guess we don't understand Russian humor.

"Anyway, Dr. Lawrence and I then discovered a cave about forty meters from the campsite. Upon entering the cave, we saw two to three mammoths. It was dark and the cave continued further down about another thirty meters. We took samples from a large mammoth that was in pristine condition. Although the anterior and posterior ends were hard to decipher, we were able to obtain a viscous sample from one of the mammoth's arteries in the leg. We hypothesise that it may in fact be blood; however, more testing, which we'll do tomorrow, will shed light on this hypothesis. After collecting the samples, we left and decontaminated near the SUV," says Dr. Fraser.

"Okay, okay. That sounds pretty routine, which is good. We don't really need any surprises," says Igor.

"So, as of right now, all we have to do is test the samples for any abnormalities," says Dr. Fraser.

"It should be a piece of cake now that we have the illustrious Dr. Igor Popov as a teammate," I say, with a bit of sarcasm.

After a mostly peaceful night's sleep, I furl my sleeping bag and change into my working man's clothes: Crocs, socks, and sweatpants. Comfort is always a priority when you're dealing with deadly pathogens.

Upon stepping outside, I realize it's a beautiful day out. The sun is shining brighter than my future, and the trees are balding faster than I am. What a great day to risk my life playing with pathogens.

Walking around the campsite through the fallen leaves, I see Dr. Fraser nervously jotting down her thoughts in her decaying brown journal.

"Mornin', sunshine," I say.

"How are you so jubilant at eight in the morning?" she asks.

"I'm a happy person. Not a care in the world. Oh, and I bet on a couple of football games last night. Let's just say, if this whole doctor thing doesn't work out, I've got a second career lined up."

"Where did you get the internet to make bets?" she asks.

"I, uh, have my ways."

"Keep your secrets. I don't care. Just know that whatever money you make, you still owe me a banana."

I scoff at her remarks and proceed with my questioning: "What time are we going to begin testing the samples today?"

"Hopefully soon. It all depends on our newly procured third wheel, Igor."

"Oh, I forgot about Papa Igor. Hey, I have a question for you. Now, I'm not one for conspiracy theories, but I've been working on one, and I want your opinion."

"Please don't tell me. I'm in no mood for a story."

"Okay, perfect. So, here it goes: a pathogen is released in an isolated setting in Siberia. Seems fine. Happens all the time, I suppose. Well, then the Russian government sets up an exclusion zone prohibiting people from leaving and getting in; however, there are visible tire treads in the mud. Seems odd, sure. Then, a scary man from a BSL-4 facility, not far from here, comes out of the blue to 'assist us.' Tell me I'm crazy, but I think this thing is deeper than a mammoth with the flu."

"Lawrence, I mean this in the nicest way possible, but you're absolutely, undeniably, incredibly crazy. I know Dr. Popov is a suspicious character; however, he's a trained professional, and I don't think Alexi really has the proper skillset. Dr. Popov is all we've got."

"Thought so. Then again, I did make a ton of money predicting football scores yesterday, so . . ."

"Just go get Igor and Alexi. We're on a time frame here."

"Okey dokie, artichokey."

I peregrinate from tent to tent looking for my Russian comrades; I find empty cots, lots of empty vodka bottles, and empty dreams. However, my search proves fruitless: no mildly intoxicated Russians. Oh, I should also mention that since Papa Igor moved into our camp, Alexi and I are no longer rooming together. They both have the whole Russian connection, and I can't compete with that.

At the moment, Alexi and Igor are currently AWOL, which is a major problem (in my view).

I peek my head back into Rebecca's tent and say: "Rebecca, we may have a problem."

"Did you run out of barbecue sauce?"

"Wait, what do you know about my barbecue sauce?"

"I'm the leader of the mission. I'm supposed to know the quirks of my subordinates."

"*Subordinates*?" I inquisitively reply.

"Anyway, what's the problem?"

"We're coming back to the condescension later, but, um, Alexi and the Papa Igor are AWOL, i.e., not in their tents."

"That's not good. Did you check to see if the cars were still here?"

"Yes, both of them are still here."

"Maybe they're by the river, relaxing or something. It is, after all, a nice day."

As we forge a path through the thick layer of mud, fallen leaves, and dirt, we see something out in the distance near the riverbank.

"Rebecca, look! I bet it's a yeti."

"You really do have the mind of a child. It's fascinating."

"At least I had a memorable childhood. Unlike you."

"Ouch. Way to assume about my childhood. Very brave."

As I get closer, I realize that it is indeed not a yeti. Disappointing, I know. Rather, it's Papa Igor using a thick, black satellite phone while Alexi throws rocks in the water, watching the ripple effect.

"Oi, oi, lads. What's up?" I enthusiastically inquire.

Igor immediately hangs up his phone and stows it into his black backpack.

"Doctors, isn't it a beautiful day out?" Igor says while standing near the riverbank. "There's no snow on the ground, the sun is shining, and the river is flowing nicely."

"Yes, indeed. Igor and I just wanted to get some fresh air, away from the smoke of the generators and the fire," says Alexi.

"Don't wander off. You could get eaten by a yeti," I reply.

"Oh, Dr. Lawrence. Do I have some stories about yetis for you," Alexi responds.

"You can tell me on the way back. Let's go."

* * *

Upon returning to the campsite, Dr. Fraser and I don our disposable scrubs and other personal protective equipment.

After we confirm the functionality of our headset and cameras with Igor, Dr. Fraser and I step inside the black shipping container into a makeshift airlock.

Once we've completed our five-minute decontamination shower, we enter the hot zone.

The bright white LED lights reflect off the corrugated steel walls, creating a sterile-looking environment. The room is smaller than you would imagine. Most of the space is taken up by the massive biosafety cabinet and the accompanying diagnostic equipment. There are two swivel chairs as well as a desk with a portable, old-school-style laptop and a pile of files.

"Hey, Rebecca. Stay safe."

"You too, Lawrence."

We immediately walk over to the biosafety cabinet, which Dr. Fraser prefilled with our samples and some basic equipment yesterday.

I should also mention that we took the utmost caution when transferring the samples into the biosafety cabinet. We followed the proper sterile techniques (called aseptic techniques in the scientific community) to ensure that no modern bacteria interacted with our samples. This would give us a greater certainty that we did not obtain a false positive—i.e., receiving a positive result for an ancient pathogen when it's really a modern one. Here's a brief rundown of what we did so far: we disinfected all surfaces (with 70 percent ethanol wipes), we wore sterile gloves when handling the samples, we limited the samples' exposure to air, and we took other more proactive measures.[16]

"Alright, Lawrence, so because I'm the trained researcher of the party and the leader, I will be conducting the majority of the tests. I know you'd had some experience in the lab, but I want you to play a more supplementary role, sort of like a research assistant. Don't do anything rash. Okay?"

"Sounds like a plan. I can do that."

"The first thing we're going to do is to see if we can actually see what we're working with," says Dr. Fraser.

"Yeah, sure. I can do that."

So, Dr. Fraser and I stick our hands into the thick gloves of the biosafety cabinet, fiddling with the light microscope that was placed inside.

"Alright, Lawrence. Can you prepare me a microscope slide with a drop of the mammoth's blood and a little bit of water while I calibrate the microscope?"

"Sure thing."

With my hands in the thick rubber gloves of the BSC, I try to pry open the Styrofoam cold box inside the cabinet. When I finally unlock the glorified cooler, I carefully take a gray pipette and obtain a minuscule amount of blood from the chilled test tube.

I whisper to myself, "don't mess up, don't mess up."

"You know I can hear you, Lawrence."

"I wasn't always the best lab partner in science class. Spilled a lot of stuff. You know the type."

"You'll be alright. I trust you."

"Aww, I wouldn't do that," I jokingly reply.

---

16 Sagar Aryal, "General Aseptic Techniques in Microbiology," *Microbe Notes* (blog), February 14, 2019.

Then, I take the pipette and eject a dollop of partially coagulated mammoth blood onto a glass microscope slide. After using another pipette to apply a drop of water, I gently apply a coverslip over the blood.

"Well, here's your slide. So what exactly is the plan? Microscopy is only a preliminary diagnostic tool, and you can't really see viruses and most bacteria on a light microscope anyway," I inquire.

"For starters, very few people have seen mammoth's blood under a microscope before. Second, although it will only give us a preliminary diagnostic, it's better than nothing. At least we can potentially narrow down our pathogen," she replies.

Dr. Fraser takes the slide from me and places it on the mechanical stage of the light microscope, securing it with the stage clip.

She cycles through the different magnifications of the microscope, playing with the course adjustment and fine adjustment nobs to focus the microscope.

Then she discovers something.

"What the hell is that?" she says.

"Wait, what? What?"

"Well, at a one thousand-times magnification, I see lots of concave red blood cells and something very, very strange."

"Strange as in 'we're all going to die' strange?" I nervously ask.

"Take a look and tell me what you see."

She pulls her hands out of the gloves and motions me over.

I comply with her demands and reposition myself in the swivel chair.

My pupils dilate, my green eyes light up, and my mouth drops.

"Wow. Wicked. I've never seen anything like that before; it's very . . ."

"Yeah, I know," she replies.

"So, is that our culprit?" I ask.

"It might be," she says.

"Well, what is it?" I ask.

"It's tough to say right now, but to me, in my honest opinion, it looks like a bunch of tiny, tiny dots among a lot of red blood cells," she says,

"So, what does that imply?" I ask.

"The speckled pattern is, well, uncommon to say the least. It could still be contamination, but we can always rule that out through more tests. In my opinion, because we can see the faintest resemblance of it, the foreign matter is probably bacterial in nature, or it may be a plasmodial infection. To push this further, we can run a litany of tests, and we'll definitely do a Gram's stain of whatever it is to increase the contrast, allowing us to get a better visual."

"I mean, it's a possibility that it's a bacterium or a plasmodium, but I wouldn't rule out a virus. Some known viruses can get that big," I reply.

"Not necessarily this big. Viruses are, generally, incredibly small. They're so small that, in fact, we can't see them with normal light microscopes. Frankly, we can't even see most bacteria until we've done a Gram's stain, which is why I want to continue testing. However, I theorise that what we're seeing, these very tiny oval-looking things, are indeed a bacteria or a plasmodia."

"Do you know what it kind of looks like?"

"Remember, this whole thing is being recorded, so don't mention anything phallic."

"I wouldn't dare, Dr. Fraser. It kind of looks like a *bursaria truncatella* that I photographed during my younger and more vulnerable years."

"That's not a bacterium or a plasmodium, but sure."

You know, this really is a shocking discovery. Dr. Fraser and I were originally under the impression that we were dealing with a virus; however, this eases most of our suspicions. Bacteria or a plasmodia aren't as bad as they sound.

This ostensible bacterium/plasmodium is really quite fascinating. It's about the same size of an *escherichia coli*, or E. coli, for the simpletons. With a size of roughly 1,500 nanometers, this thing is still incredibly small. At a magnification of one thousand times using a high-tech light microscope, it's barely visible. Like I mentioned earlier, they just look like very faint dots that are dwarfed by the mammoth's concave-looking red blood cells. However, it's there, which effectively rules out most, if not all, lethal viruses.[17]

"Look at us, who would've thought? A bacterium or an angry little plasmodium did all of this. Crazy," I say.

"Now, let's not count our spores before they fertilise. We still need to run more tests," Dr. Fraser says.

"That joke doesn't land."

"Dr. Lancaster would've found it funny," she replies.

"Nobody finds that funny."

"A sense of humor doesn't hurt, you know," she says.

"*You're* telling *me* about a sense of humor? I need to retire."

"You're, what, like, in your mid-thirties? You aren't going to retire anytime soon."

"A man can dream, Rebecca. What's next then?"

---

17   Petra Anne Levin and Esther R. Angert, "Small but Mighty: Cell Size and Bacteria," *Cold Spring Harbor Perspectives in Biology* 7, no. 7 (July 2015).

"Well, to determine if this mammoth had bacteraemia, or bacteria in the bloodstream, we need to effectively culture or reproduce the bacteria. Your job is to take a small amount of blood and place it into these BD BACTEC medium bottles," she says.[18]

"I can do that, but might I ask: Why do we need the bottles? I haven't cultured bacteria since freshman year of college, and we didn't use the bottles. We just used agar."

"Right. Um, the bottles contain a special medium that is enriched with nutrients and various growth factors that spur the growth and reproduction of bacteria. This is what we, in the research community, like to call blood culture by broth method. In theory, the plan goes like this: we add the blood to the BACTEC medium, we place the bottles into a BACTEC analyser, and then we get results back in a couple of days."

Following Dr. Fraser's marching orders, I cautiously use the pipette to transfer approximately eight milliliters of mammoth blood into the aerobic BACTEC broth bottle. This, Dr. Fraser assures me, will detect any bacteria that grow in the presence of oxygen. Additionally, she also has me prepare a bottle using an anaerobic medium, which will allow bacteria that grow in the absence of oxygen to grow.[19]

---

18   Angela M Minassian et al., "Use of an Automated Blood Culture System (BD BACTEC) for Diagnosis of Prosthetic Joint Infections: Easy and Fast," *BMC Infectious Diseases 14,* (May 2013): 233.

19   Rita Passerini et al., "Recovery and Time to Growth of Isolates in Blood Culture Bottles: Comparison of BD Bactec Plus Aerobic/F and BD Bactec Plus Anaerobic/F Bottles," *Scandinavian Journal of Infectious Diseases 46,* no. 4 (April 2014): 288-293.

"Boom. Here you go, ma'am. Two bottles of Dr. Lawrence's finest. One is a nice red wine, imported from the far land of Siberia, and the other is a domestic red wine produced by me."

"You could've just handed me the bottles sans commentary, but instead you go the goofball route."

"I'm a physician, not a researcher. A comedian, not a goofball. I'm here to diagnose and treat illnesses caused by the pathogen, not study it," I reply.

I hand off my life's work, and Dr. Fraser opens the door of the portable BACTEC analyzer machine. After that, she places each of the two bottles into one of the four perfectly sized holes. Then, she fidgets with the settings until the machine lets out an audible "beep."

"Now, the bottles containing our blood samples will sit in this fancy machine, which is a BACTEC analyser. All it does is incubate the samples at thirty-five degrees Celsius and rotate the bottle to encourage growth," she says.

"Sweet. How long is the whole process going to take? It's getting kind of hot in here."

Sweat starts to bead up on my forehead, dripping down on the clear glass window of the biosafety cabinet.

"I know. I noticed that. Um, it depends. It depends on the bacteria in the sample. If they are present, the bacteria should metabolise the nutrients in the broth, which will release carbon dioxide. That's basic respiration. Now, this fancy machine actually detects carbon dioxide with sensors and what not. Then, it transmits that data over to Igor's computer screen outside, which should tell us if carbon dioxide has been produced. To answer your question more directly, we can check back tomorrow, and we should have some growth to inoculate onto solid media."

"Wham, bam, thank you, ma'am. That means I'm done for the day."

She rolls her eyes and exhales loudly.

Then she says, "We can't really do anything until we get the test results back, so yes, we are indeed done for today."

Dehydrated and drenched in sweat, Dr. Fraser and I enter the makeshift airlock and undergo our seven-minute chemical decontamination shower. Once our chemical ablutions are finished, we take a secondary personal shower in order to fully disinfect our persons.

Upon exiting the literal "hot zone," Papa Igor and my man, Alexi, approach us in an inquisitive manner.

"So, doctors, how was it? What did you see?" asks Igor.

"It went well. Dr. Lawrence was a wonderful but tricky assistant. In regard to the actual sampling, we have a preliminary hypothesis."

"Wonderful. What is your consensus?" asks Alexi.

"At the moment, Dr. Lawrence and I, after consulting merely microscopic evidence, believe that our pathogen is a bacterium or a plasmodium, not a virus. To confirm this, we have set up a blood culture using the broth method, and after those preliminary results, we will utilise solid media such as agar in order to confirm our hypothesis," says Dr. Fraser.

"Alright, so what's the plan for the rest of the day?" asks Alexi.

"Not much. Our preliminary tests should be completed by tomorrow, and then we can start the antibiotic trials. Meanwhile, I'll go update Dr. Lancaster on what we've discovered today," says Dr. Fraser.

Dr. Fraser retreats into her tent while Alexi and Igor migrate to another quadrant of the camp, leaving me alone outside of the makeshift BSL-4 facility.

There's only one thing on my mind: How on earth did Dr. Fraser find out about my barbecue sauce?

The next day brings with it a whirlwind of emotions.

My no longer "secret" stash of barbecue sauce is slowly draining, and I have to go back inside the BSL-4 to inspect our bacteria.

I grudgingly slide out of my sleeping bag and perform my morning stretches. With my muscles flexed and relaxed, I exit my tent, letting out an audible yawn for the whole world to hear.

"Good morning, Lawrence," says Dr. Fraser.

"It's too early for pleasantries," I shout.

"It's eleven o'clock."

I walk over to the smoldering campfire where Dr. Fraser is sitting on a collapsible chair.

My eyes widen, "Really? How long did I sleep?"

"Rough night?" she asks.

"You can say that. I made some realizations about my future last night."

"Fun. You're not as energetic, so it mustn't be good news."

"You can say that."

"Do you know what will cheer you up?" she says.

"I swear to God, if you say anything referencing pathogens, bacteria, Mini Coopers, squid, or mammoths, I'm going to quit."

"A nice chemical shower should cheer you up."

I let out an audible groan that sounds like a baby bear when it scratches its back against a tree. It's a real sight to see if you've never seen it.

Upon retrieving some bland coffee, I return to my temporary domicile, the collapsible tent. I plop myself down on my cot and eventually contain my marbles. I basically give myself a motivational speech, sort of like a YouTube entrepreneurship channel would. It goes something like this: "Yesterday is history, tomorrow is a mystery, and today is a present. Blah blah blah. You can do anything. . . ."

With my ducks in a metaphorical row, I reacquaint myself with Dr. Fraser and we enter into the BSL-4 facility.

"Alright, what's on today's agenda?" I ask.

"Well, we need to check the BACTEC analyser to see if our samples created a positive result, implying the presence of bacteria in the mammoth's blood. Then, as an extra test, we're going to attempt to culture the bacteria on solid media."

"Wicked fun."

"Oh, someone finally turned their mood around."

I scoff at her sarcastic comments and finish doing my routine chores.

Dr. Fraser checks the computer monitors on the laptop inside of the shipping container, presumably to check the carbon dioxide production in the bottles.

"That's weird," she says.

"What? Did I mess up?"

"Maybe, but the machine is most likely not functioning properly."

"How so?"

"Well, it's saying that no carbon dioxide was produced in the bottles. Both samples, the aerobic and the anaerobic, produced negative results. You see, the stagnant, or flat line, shows that carbon dioxide production was nonexistent. In theory, because it's a bacterium, it should be producing an exponential graph, showing increasing levels of carbon dioxide production."

"What if the bacteria are . . . what's the correct scientific word? Picky?" I ask.

"Fastidious?"

"Yes!" I swivel around in the chair.

"They could be fastidious bacteria that only grow in the presence of certain nutrients. We'll most likely have to test the mammoth's blood on several different types of solid media instead. I do still have one more trick up my sleeve for liquid media."

"Well, what's your trick?"

"Robertson's cooked meat."

"Hold up. Should I go get my barbecue sauce? Are we having a feast?" I respond.

Alexi chimes in over the intercom: "Are the doctors having a feast without us?"

"No, no, no. Robertson's cooked meat is a type of liquid media, sort of like a broth. It's basically sterilised cooked meat that scientists use to grow fastidious bacteria. We'll still have to transplant it on solid media, but it should improve our sensitivity and yield of the culture," she replies.[20]

Following Dr. Fraser's orders, I prepare one vial of Robertson's cooked meat with one drop of mammoth's blood.

In regard to solid media, there are several different types; however, for simplicity's sake, I'll mention three of the varieties we're going to use (although we're going to use a lot more).

20　Acharya Tankeshwar, "Robertson's Cooked Meat (RCM) Medium: Principle, Composition, Procedure and Uses," *Microbe Online* (blog), November 29, 2016.

In general, solid media culture involves the use of a petri dish and a Jell-O-like substance called agar, which is made from seaweed. Interesting, I know.

The first type of solid media culture is basal media, which is, in my opinion, the simplest type of solid media. It's purely agar that is enhanced with nutrients such as glucose, salts, and beef extract, among others. Unfortunately, this type of media is great for non-fastidious bacteria, like our friend E. coli, but it isn't the best for fastidious bacteria, like the mammoth's ostensible bacteria.[21]

The second type of solid media is known as enriched media, and like the name implies it's, well, enriched. It's enriched with substances that encourage the growth of more fastidious organisms. For instance, enriched media can be modulated to express a certain pH. Our agar that we're using is enriched with 5 percent sheep's blood, which should create a goldilocks type of environment for the bacteria.[22]

Finally, the third type of media I've elected to explain is called MacConkey agar. It's the pickiest of them all. It's selective and differential. It has these properties because it contains a special type of salt, called bile salt, which will inhibit the growth of many bacteria. Only a special type of bacteria can grow on MacConkey's agar, specifically gram-negative bacteria.[23]

---

21   Acharya Tankeshwar, "Bacterial Culture Media: Classification, Types, and Uses," *Microbe Online* (blog), July 24, 2016.

22   M. Bonnet et al., "Bacterial Culture Through Selective and Non-Selective Conditions: The Evolution of Culture Media in Clinical Microbiology," *New Microbes and New Infections* 34, (November 2019).

23   Kenneth Smith, "The Origin of MacConkey Agar," American Society for Microbiology, October 14, 2019.

The difference between gram-negative and gram-positive bacteria is a story for another day, but here's the brief synopsis: Gram-positive bacteria have thick cell walls, which pick up a greater stain, leading to a much darker color. Gram-negative bacteria only have a very thin cell wall, which means they won't stain as much. The staining allows us to visualize the bacteria, and it also allows us to classify them.[24]

Now that the tricky science is out of the way, Dr. Fraser and I start preparing the petri dishes with our samples.

"Alright, you're going to remove a sample of blood from the BACTEC bottle and smear it over the agar petri dishes in a four-quadrant pattern. Can you do that?" Dr. Fraser demands.

"Sure. What are you going to do while I labor?"

"I'm going to gram stain the sample to see if our bacteria are gram-negative or gram-positive. In case you don't know, gram-positive is . . ."

I cut her off, "Rebecca, you don't need to explain everything to me. I know about Gram's stains."

"Well, alrighty then. Let the staining begin."

I start to smear the aqueous solution from the bottles on our solid media. Meanwhile, Dr. Fraser uses the light microscope to do a Gram's stain of the solution.

"Huh, that's weird," she adds.

"Again. I'm starting to doubt your authoritarian style of leadership. What is it now?"

"The staining test is, well, not working. It's not staining anything."

---

24 Karen Steward, "Gram Positive vs Gram Negative," Technology Networks, August 21, 2019.

"Well, we always have MacConkey's test, so it shouldn't be the end of the world. It may just be the fastidious nature of the bacteria messing with us . . . again," I reply.

"That's true."

* * *

Eventually, with the help of Dr. Fraser, I finish inoculating the blood onto the agar petri dishes.

"Alright, unfortunately, we're at the mercy of time again. Bacteria are tricky organisms, and culturing them requires at least a day, maybe more; however, we should see the initial results tomorrow," she says.

"Unless something goes wrong . . . again," I add.

And boy, does something go wrong. It goes very wrong.

The next day, Dr. Fraser and I decide to check up on our fastidious little friends in the biosafety cabinet.

"Lawrence, I have no clue what we're doing wrong. Nothing is growing. Nothing. MacConkey's agar is blank; The basal media is blank; and the enriched media is, well, blank. Even Robertson's cooked meat, which pretty much works on everything, is blank," Dr. Fraser says.

"I know it wasn't me. I streaked each petri dish with a drop of blood, and then I let them incubate upside down to avoid condensation buildup." I reply.

"I know, I know. The bacteria could be dead. Usually dead bacteria look the same as live bacteria, so that could be it. But wait, how could it infect the tuskers if it were dead? I think I'm losing my mind," she says.

"Maybe you're wrong. Maybe we're both wrong. Maybe it's not a bacter—"

She butts in: "That's mostly impossible."

"Wait, just hear me out for a second. It could be a virus; Gram's stains won't detect a virus because viruses don't have cell walls. Viruses also can't grow in the presence of an agar solution. They need a host, so it may be a virus."

She shakes her head in defiance and looks in the opposite direction, toward the biosafety cabinet.

"Let me explain further. I, as you may know, am an avid reader of the *National Geographic*. I read an article a couple of years ago."

"And? Your point?" she says.

"Just wait, just wait. Now, the article was about giant viruses."

"Giant what?"

"Giant viruses? Have you seriously never heard of these before? Do I know something that Dr. Fraser doesn't know?"

"I've probably heard of them before. I do a lot of reading as well. However, I usually stick to, well, scientific papers and not news sites."

"I'm going to need a moment. I feel a rush of dopamine entering my brain right now. Wow, is this how you feel all the time?"

"Alright, Lawrence. Back to reality. What's a giant virus?"

"So, giant viruses. I think the article talked about *pandoraviruses* and *pithoviruses*. Anyway, they are a type of virus that you can see under a microscope. Now, the article said that these bad boys are incredibly rare, which is why it didn't even cross my mind until now. However, if my memory serves me correctly, a French team found some of these giant viruses located in Siberia, of all places. I'm not saying the sample that we found is a *pandoravirus* or *pithovirus*. The French scientists said those varieties mainly feed on amoebas. Ours feeds on, well, humans, so I think we may have discovered something different. Still, their size is very comparable, so it's a possibility. Other than that, I have no clue. Maybe a prion or a plasmodium?"[25]

Dr. Fraser stands there defeated. She is flabbergasted.

"I can't believe I'm about to admit this, but Dr. Lawrence, you're probably right, barbecue sauce and all."

I tilt my head and say, "Thanks, I guess."

"Alright, so the next step for us is to unravel the aetiology of our supposed novel virus. What else did the article say about these giant viruses?" asks Dr. Fraser

"Well, for starters, they are big boys; they have a lot of genes. HIV for instance has twelve genes; Ebola has seven genes; *pandoraviruses* have upward of 2,500. Second, it also said that they're built like tanks. Their incredible genetic blueprint codes for a variety of different traits, like extreme toughness, which explains why they are able to survive these extreme temperatures," I say.[26]

"The first step should be to trace the genome of our supposed virus. To do that, we'll do . . ."

Igor chimes in over the intercom: "Dr. Fraser, Dr. Lancaster is on the line. He says it's urgent."

"Patch him through to my headset," she says.

I stand there, staring into Dr. Fraser's face.

"We have a what now?" she says.

---

25   Nadav Brandes and Michal Linial, "Giant Viruses—Big Surprises," *Viruses* 11, no. 5 (April 2019).

26   Stefan Sirucek, "Ancient 'Giant Virus' Revived from Siberian Permafrost," March, 2014.

Her facial features immediately start to tense up.

"Really? How is that possible?" she replies.

She puts her hand to her forehead and starts to rub it.

After a brief amount of time on the call, Dr. Lancaster hangs up, and Dr. Fraser turns to me.

"We have another problem, and it's a pretty big one," she says.

CHAPTER 7:

PATIENT ZERO

———

"What's the damage? Are we out of a job?" I jokingly ask.

"Dr. Lancaster says that a hospital in Moscow received a patient a few hours ago. . . ."

"Oh no," I butt in.

"I know. The hospital staff said the man is in his early thirties. He apparently came in and was complaining about a lot of strange symptoms: swelling, severe pain in the chest, trouble breathing, and seizures, and he was coughing up blood."

"I mean, it could be a heart attack. Odd, sure. But I've seen young people have heart attacks before. The coughing up blood is a strange side effect, but you never know nowadays."

"It wasn't a heart attack," she says.

"Really?" I stop swiveling in the chair.

I stand up and start pacing around the narrow corridor of the BSL-4 facility.

"The doctors think it's something else, and get this, Dr. Lancaster told me that the man drove up from Siberia where he worked at a 'mine.' Now, Dr. Lancaster did not explain what a 'mine' meant, but I think we may have our first index case."

I start rubbing my fingers through my hair as I contemplate what's about to happen.

"Alright . . . alright . . . alright." I calmly say to myself. "What do you want to do now? Do you want to start sequencing the genome of our new child, the novel *pleistovirus,* or should we pack up and go check up on our index case in Moscow?"

"Wait a minute. . . . Before I decide anything, did you seriously give it a name?" Dr. Fraser asks.

"Yeah. What's wrong with that?"

"Lawrence, it's not a stray dog. You can't just give it a name and call it your own. Besides, there's protocol for naming a new virus, and I'm pretty sure tacking on a random word to 'virus' doesn't make it legitimate."

"Pleistocene. It's not a random word. It's the name of the timeframe when mammoths lived."

"No. That's not how it works," she says, rather sternly. "There are rules. There's a committee. It's diplomatic. For instance, the International Committee on Taxonomy of Viruses stipulates that the name of the virus shall not consist only of a host name and the word 'virus,' and . . ."[27]

"I didn't call it a *mammothovirus.*"

"Alright, well the name should only consist of as few words as practicable but be distinct from names of other taxa."

"I think you're just mad because I created an incredibly unique name that's also cool and practical. Besides, I decided not to name it a *Siberovirus* because, well, it's in poor taste."

---

27   "The International Code of Virus Classification and Nomenclature," International Committee on Taxonomy of Viruses, Date Accessed October 10, 2020.

"Explain your logic, please," Dr. Fraser says as she starts stacking up the files on the desk.

"Well, I don't want Siberians to get a negative rap for having a virus named after themselves. By naming a virus after the town or state or province it was discovered in, we are virtually ostracizing a whole community who most likely don't even know that this thing exists. For instance, let's take good ol' Brisbane. In the early 1990s, a researcher discovered a novel virus just north of the city in a town called Hendra in Queensland. Now, they, after much discussion, settled on the name of the *Hendravirus*. It may not mean much to you and to me, but the people of Hendra, Australia, now cope with the negative stigma created by the virus—the point being I did my homework on this one. Trust me."[28]

"That's what happened with Marburg," she says as she starts packing the pens and pencils into a pouch.

"Exactly," I reply.

With the conversation stalled, we start packing up our belongings in a slow and smooth fashion. The lone ten-foot desk is now barren, sans papers, pencils, or a laptop.

Next, we focus our attention on the biosafety cabinet.

Using the thick rubber gloves of the BSC, she neatly organizes the remaining test tubes and pipettes in a row.

"You know, I wanted to call it a *Rebeccovirus* in honor of you, but I don't think you'd want your name plastered all over CNN by the time this thing becomes a pandemic."

"How kind. And they say chivalry is dead," she says.

Dr. Fraser is preparing for our departure. We are evacuating. She loads pretty much everything—the remaining

---

28   David Quammen, *Spillover: Animal Infections and the Next Human Pandemic* (New York: W. W. Norton & Company, 2012): 14-34.

samples, all our used test tubes, and anything that was exposed—into the autoclave system, which will effectively disinfect the supplies. With our index case experiencing life-threatening systems, it's usually a good idea to move with a bit of purpose.

"Anyway, why no sequencing?" I say as I lean back in the swivel chair.

"Dr. Lancaster wants us to make the trip to Moscow."

"That makes sense."

"The main reason he wants us there is because he doesn't trust the Russian government to give an accurate report of the incident. We haven't found any bodies yet, so we don't know how it interacts with the human body. He wants you to catalog the symptoms and see if any known antivirals will abate any of it."

"I can do that. Do you need me to do anything, or is this a typical CIA-style 'burn everything and leave' type of mission?" I inquire.

With a tilt of the head, Dr. Fraser turns and stares directly in my eyes.

"Staring contest? Really, Rebecca? In this mess?"

"No. Your eyes are bloodshot. It's like a red spider web is covering your whole sclera in both of your eyes."

"Like I said, I was tired," I shrug off her comments.

"Lawrence, I don't think so. I think there's something wrong . . ."

"I'm fine!" I angrily reply. "I haven't been sleeping well. Okay?"

"What's wrong?" she asks.

"I'm surprised that you can sleep through all of this. With everything going on, it really gets at your insides."

"In what way?"

"I don't know." I shrug my shoulders and walk away toward the lone plexiglass window. "I've had some chest pains, but I don't think it's too serious."

"Where?" she asks.

I use my right hand to point to every nook and cranny of my chest. "Here. Here. Here."

"Are you sure it's nothing?"

"Yeah. Totally, I probably just slept on it wrong. These cots aren't the most comfortable thing in the world."

"But you haven't slept. Do you see the problem?"

"No," I frankly reply.

"We're going to check up on that when we get to Moscow," she demands.

"Did Alexi and Papa Igor hear our conversation?" I ask

We both peer through the plexiglass window, looking at our friendly Russian comrades smoking outside of the facility. They were, thankfully, not paying attention to anything that happened in the past several minutes.

Igor and Alexi are standing with their backs turned, pointing at trees and laughing. They were simply socializing, presumably making fun of my Crocs and socks.

"Don't worry about the sequencing though. I sent some blood samples to other labs a couple of days ago," she says.

"Wait, when did you do that? I was here the whole time."

"I woke up early a couple of days ago."

"Oh. That's why Dr. Lancaster put you in charge. I got it," I reply. "But don't we have time to at least start the sequencing though?" I ask.

"We don't really have the equipment. Plus, it will take too long," she asks.

"I thought we had a PCR machine, and we have a couple of hours," I respond.

"Well, it takes more time than that. A lot of time. We could probably sequence a couple of genes here and there, but to sequence the whole genome, it'll take a couple more than a couple of hours," she says.

"It's been far too long since I've sequenced anything."

"I can reexplain it for you if you want."

"Oh, no. No, I don't think I'll . . ."

"Great. So, the main components are centrifugation and PCR sequencing," she says.

I immediately let out a groan in protest, but I eventually acquiesce and listen to her pontifications.

"Now, centrifugation's purpose is to separate the virus, or even antibodies, from the actual blood. It uses speed and centripetal forces to isolate particles by shape, size, and density. The labs may take advantage of a relatively new method of centrifugation called ultracentrifugation, which uses a very high centripetal force to separate very small particles; however, because we're dealing with the novel, I can't believe I'm going to say it, *pleistovirus* . . ."[29]

"See, it's got a nice ring to it!" I shake my head and flail my arms outward.

"I guess it does. Where was I? Anyway, from there, the labs can also choose to culture and isolate the virus. Now, because viruses require a living host cell to replicate, they need living cells in order to be cultured and isolated in a lab. They'll most likely choose to grow these cells in vitro, meaning in a cell outside of a living organism, most likely in a test tube or petri dish, but it gets much, much more complicated than that. For instance, viruses are surprisingly picky and don't like to be

---

29   C.J. Peters and Mark Olshaker, *Virus Hunter: Thirty Years of Battling Hot Viruses Around the World* (New York: Anchor Books, 1998): 216.

cultured in certain cells, so they'll most likely use a whole host of cells. Cells from a dog's kidney, rat tumor cells, cells from rhesus monkeys, and even human fetus cells can all be used to grow viruses. Now, once the virus proliferates, it will usually kill the living cells in a process called the cytopathic effect. At this point, we can usually start to study how the virus interacts with a host—via electron microscopes—and we can gain clues about its mechanisms and functions. The point is viruses are harder to culture than bacteria, and it would take a long time for a single lab to isolate and culture the virus."[30]

"That makes sense, but you forgot about the actual sequencing part. Just saying. . . ."

"I thought you weren't listening?" she asks.

"Rebecca, I'm enthralled by your story. You can't just end it on a cliff hanger. How do we go from a viral culture to a genetic sequence?"

"I'll make this quick, but then we have to go get Alexi and Igor," she says as she rubs her forehead. "Um, DNA and RNA viral sequencing trace their roots back to PCR testing, otherwise known as polymerase chain reactions. Now, PCR testing has been a fundamental process for the past several decades. However, it was revolutionized in the late 1970s with the introduction of Sanger sequencing, which allows us to get snippets of the actual genome. Back in the old days, Sanger sequencing was used for everything: viral genomes, animal genomes, and scientists even sequenced the human genome in 2003. However, the cost is usually astronomical, which is why it's been replaced by a newer, faster method called next-generation sequencing, or NGS. Fortunately, PCR is

---

30   Quammen, *Spillover,* 184-185.

pretty much a mainstay of all the different methods, so I'll focus my explanation on that," Dr. Fraser says.[31]

"Now, I'm going to preface my explanation by assuming that our *pleistovirus* is a DNA virus mostly because *pandoraviruses* and *pithoviruses* are DNA viruses as well."

"I wouldn't assume it's a DNA virus," I reply. "DNA viruses imply stability; DNA viruses don't usually spillover between reservoir hosts, intermediate hosts, and humans. Their genetic sequence doesn't mutate that much, so I would assume our virus is RNA based."[32]

"For the record, you are probably correct, Lawrence. The labs I sent the samples to will run a bunch of tests to determine if it is indeed an RNA virus. However, to simplify my explanation, I'll assume that it's DNA-based.

"Now, back to the topic at hand: Sanger sequencing. Although it's arcane and isn't used much anymore, it still works. It uses a DNA polymerase enzyme, which adds nucleotides. It also uses a primer, which acts as a starting point for DNA replication, i.e. where the nucleotides are added. Additionally, the process utilises all four nucleotides—adenine, thymine, guanine, and cytosine. Finally, it also contains special variants of the nucleotides, called dideoxynucleotides, or dNTPs, which prevent DNA polymerase from adding nucleotides to it, thus stopping elongation."

Like a deer in headlights, I stand there, starring into her face.

"Didee what now?" I ask.

---

31   James Heather and Benjamin Chain, "The Sequence of Sequencers: The History of Sequencing DNA," *Genomics 107*, no. 1 (January 2016): 1-8.

32   Alan Dove, "Shotgunning the Messenger: Single-Cell RNA Sequencing," *Science,* February 21, 2019.

"Dideoxynucleotides. They're basically a stop sign. Whenever DNA polymerase, the enzyme that adds nucleotides onto the primer, reaches a dideoxynucleotide, it stops."

"Ah, okay, okay. They didn't teach us that in medical school. We learned about polymerase chain reactions, but not Sanger sequencing," I reply

"Yeah, the process nowadays is pretty similar to PCR testing: you add the DNA, the primers, the nucleotides, and the DNA polymerase in a tube and use a PCR machine. The basic process is simple. It's sort of like the copy and paste command on a computer. First, it heats the tube, which denatures the DNA, causing the strands to separate. Then, the primers bind to aspecific area on one of the split DNA strands. It's sort of like a specific Lego piece binding to another specific Lego piece."

"You have a way with analogies, Rebecca," I interlude.

She smirks and continues, "I really do. Um. After that, DNA polymerase works its magic, adding nucleotides. These nucleotides are added in a complementary format: Adenine binds to thymine and guanine to cytosine. Now, here comes the fun part. If DNA polymerase happens to add a dNTP, the elongation of the replicated DNA strand stops, ending with the dNTP. The whole process hits a stop sign. This happens in a controlled setting, and it can go on for hours through thousands of cycles until every nucleotide in that section of DNA is replicated.

"Now, once the process is finished, usually after a couple of hours or maybe even a couple of days, the replicated DNA fragments go through gel electrophoresis. All gel electrophoresis does is separate the shortened fragments by length, meaning that a fragment with ten nucleotides will be read before a fragment with one hundred nucleotides. It's incredibly, incredibly accurate, and a laser-like machine will read staining of the dNTPs at the end of the fragment. After each fragment has been recorded, it produces a chromatogram, which displays the exact sequence of that particular strand of DNA."[33]

"That's how I remember doing it many moons ago. Time, time, and more time," I reply.

"Exactly, and that's why we can't do it. Nowadays, most labs do faster and cheaper methods of genome sequencing like next-generation sequencing, NGS. These methods are much, much cheaper and incredibly fast. However, the most important difference between Sanger sequencing and NGS is that NGS gives you the full genome, whereas Sanger sequencing gives you one or two genes, not the full genome. Additionally, Sanger sequencing relies on preexisting primers, which can be hard to come by when you're dealing with a novel virus. However, in my opinion, nothing will truly replace the simplicity of PCR reactions. All it does is copy DNA and RNA over and over.[34]

"Oh . . . one more thing that I forgot to mention. Knowing the genetic sequence of a virus isn't entirely important early on, so we can still do our work tracking the pathogen. The genetic sequence will tell us how many genes the *pleistovirus* has, but it won't tell us what they do or how they interact with our immune system."

---

33   Jeremy Schoales, "How Does Sanger Sequencing Work?" *ThermoFisher Scientific* (blog), June 17, 2015.

34   Sam Behajti and Patrick S. Tarpey, "What Is Next Generation Sequencing?" *Archives of Disease in Childhood. Education and Practice Edition* 98, no. 6 (December 2013): 236-238.

"Well, I wouldn't say they're useless. Right? They contain the amino acids, which code for the proteins," I ask.

"I didn't say they were *useless.* I said they were pretty much useless to us right now. They're mostly used for making vaccines and antivirals. Knowing the genetic sequence can speed up the manufacturing process for vaccines, leading to a more effective vaccine. However, vaccines usually take years to develop, so if this virus becomes a pandemic, we're most likely going to have to wait on a vaccine," she says.

"So, not to interrupt your splendiferous pontifications, but when are we rolling out like the Autobots?"

"You did not just use the words splendiferous, pontifications, and Autobots in the same sentence."

I shrug my shoulders and let out a little smirk, admitting my quirkiness.

"Well, we're going to have to break the news to Dr. Popov and Alexi. Dr. Popov isn't going to like the idea that he has to stay here and take over the lab while we're gone."

* * *

Dr. Fraser and I go through our decontamination processes and exit the laboratory only to be met by a concerned Papa Igor and Alexi.

Immediately upon exiting the black shipping container, Alexi flags us down and starts pacing in our general direction.

"Big problems ahead," Alexi shouts.

"What do you mean big problems ahead? I thought the Russians have this *pleistovirus* under control?" I ask.

Alexi cocks his head to the side and gapes his mouth open, ostensibly trying to translate from Russian.

"Wait, what's the problem?" I ask again.

"What is this *pleistovirus*?" Alexi asks.

Igor appears from behind the shipping container with the black satellite phone in his hands and his arms crossed.

"Well, it's Dr. Lawrence's unique and colourful name for this new pathogen, pending approval from the Dr. Lancaster and the International Committee on Taxonomy of Viruses, of course," says Dr. Fraser.

"Again, what's the problem?" I ask.

"I think it would be better if we get out of the weather and go to the makeshift control center," says Igor Popov.

The four of us perambulate through the viscous mud to the control center, leaving a visible trail in our wake.

* * *

"Much better. There is less mud and filth in here," says Igor.

"We keep it tidy," I reply.

"So, what's the problem?" Dr. Fraser asks.

"Here is the problem: we believe one of the tuskers breached our impenetrable exclusion zone and made his way to Moscow. How he got to Moscow, we do not know. We also do not know whom he talked to, or why he went to Moscow first," says Alexi.

"So, you're telling us that the impenetrable Maginot Line-esque exclusion zone was broken by a man who wanted to make a quick buck by selling some bones?" I ask with a tilt of the head.

"It seems that way, doctors." Alexi fiddles with his fingers, avoiding eye contact.

Here's the thing: Dr. Fraser and I realize they're still not giving us the full picture of what's going on, so why trust them? For the time being, we're going to play dumb and see where it goes. We may end up staying in Siberia forever (not fun), or we may crack the case of this cold-hearted virus.

"Well, I need to be there to observe the effects of this virus," I say.

"I agree with Dr. Lawrence on this one. Now, we can't assume that the virus is controlled. The index case may have used airplanes to travel, or he may have made some illicit, black- market deals in Moscow. It could be around the world by now. The best thing we can do right now is understand how it interacts with living human cells so we can understand how to treat it. Lawrence, go upload our preliminary research to the predict database as well as the gene bank."

"Sure thing," I reply.

After I finish uploading our data to the interweb, we're ready to depart. How long did I take to transfer a couple of files? I guess time flies when you can't read a watch.

I load my military-grade backpack and a couple of small supply crates into Igor's Soviet-era red SUV while Dr. Fraser talks on the phone.

Taking one last look at the Siberian wilderness, I realize I never want to come back. Even though it's Siberia, it gets pretty hot, and you sweat a lot, especially when you're wearing a glorified garbage bag while collecting samples in a cave.

Dr. Fraser hangs up the phone and trudges through the mud back to the SUV. She wipes the mud that's caked on her shoes and opens the rear door, creating a loud screeching sound. She then plops into the back seat of the SUV next to me and my backpack.

"Okay, that phone call went mildly well," Dr. Fraser says as she slams the door.

"What did Dr. Lancaster have to say?" I ask.

"Oh, that wasn't Dr. Lancaster. Nope. It was the head of the World Health Organization, and before you ask, I gave her our preliminary name of the virus."

"Well . . . did she describe the name as a literary masterpiece?" I ask.

"She liked it, and she even used it in a press conference today, so . . ."

"So, we're celebrities among the microbiologists and virologists."

"I can't tell if you're being facetious or not," she replies.

"What else did she say?"

"She kept it short. She said that she has press conferences and briefings lined up for the whole day. She also said the samples that we sent to other labs are being sequenced as we speak via illumina sequencing, a type of next-generation sequencing. With that being said, it's all up to your medical school degree to get us through the next hurdle," she says.

"Oh, boy. God help us, we're in the hands of a poorly trained physician."

We both look at each other, realizing the utter shitstorm we're about to enter. There's nothing to say. We only purse our lips and nod.

Drifting away from reality, I decide to look out the window and notice something incredibly odd. It's not a Mini Cooper, nor is it a mini Bradley Cooper. It's a man and a child walking through a thicket of bushes and broken tree limbs. Unfortunately, because of Alexi's reckless driving, I couldn't get an accurate description of who they were or what they were doing.

"Yo, Alexi, my man. Call me crazy, but I think, bear with me, I think I just saw a man and a small child walking through the forest."

"Really? Where?" Dr. Fraser asks.

"They were back there. About three hundred meters yonder." I point east out the car window.

"Well, there's a village that's not too far from here. They're probably just taking a hike. Nothing more," says Alexi.

"I understand that, but what happened to the whole exclusion zone thing? Was that just a farce, or . . ." I ask.

"No, no," Alexi asserts. "The exclusion zone is very much intact. Those people are from a village that's not too far away. It's a tiny village. They mostly keep to themselves, and they don't interact with the outside world too much. The Russian military set up the perimeter around the tusking site, not our campsite, so that explains where they are closer to us."

Alexi tries to change the topic from the Russian containment efforts to something uniquely bizarre.

"I have a story about that village. Do you want to hear it?" Alexi asks.

Again, Dr. Fraser and I just turn to each other in the backset and shake our heads in protest.

"Wonderful. Well, that town has a unique history of bad things happening to it. My favorite story about that town involves a child, anthrax, and reindeer."

"I'm intrigued yet frightened, Alexi," I add.

"Yes. Back in the early 1940s, scientists think a reindeer died near that village. Now, when it died, anthrax spores basically nested inside of its body. At the time, it was fine, because the carcass was covered in several feet of permafrost. However, in recent years, with the climate changing and all, the permafrost melted, and a couple of years ago the frozen carcass was exposed. The exposed carcass more or less melted, and the anthrax spores found their way into a river. Here's where it gets interesting. A herd of reindeer drank from that water and about two thousand of them became infected."[35]

"Wow. Two thousand? Hopefully Rudolph wasn't one of them," I interject.

"Oh, yes. A full two thousand. In fact, this has become commonplace in Siberia. In 2016, in a separate incident, I think, a boy stumbled upon another frozen reindeer that had been unearthed by thawing permafrost. Unfortunately, the boy passed away and at least twenty villagers were hospitalized after anthrax found its way into the village, but scientists think that this may become a common phenomenon as the permafrost continues to thaw," says Alexi.[36]

Eating Tim Tams, I reply: "Jesus. It just makes you think about what else is out there."

With Alexi's monologue ending, the sound of silence quickly engulfs the car, and Dr. Fraser and I rest our eyes for the remainder of the voyage.

"Okay, doctors. We're here," Alexi says in a soft and gentle voice.

Still half asleep, Dr. Fraser and I haphazardly stumble out of the parked SUV onto the runway.

Feeling clunky and perturbed, I perform several yoga poses and stretches to ease any built-up tension. Nothing fancy. Just a couple of standard poses—the downward dog and the starving artist.

---

35 Melody Schreiber, "The Next Pandemic Could Be Hiding in the Arctic Permafrost," *New Republic*, April 2, 2020.

36 Jasmin Fox-Skelly, "There Are Diseases Hidden in Ice, and They Are Waking Up," *BBC*, May 4, 2017.

While I stand there, taking in the picturesque scenery of cracking concrete, Dr. Fraser and Alexi unload the supplies from the trunk of the car, setting them on the tarmac.

"Alright, let's get this show on the road," I say.

"Technically, we're not going on the road. We're going in the air," says Dr. Fraser.

I let out a groan as I slam the car's door shut.

"Enough playing, doctors. We have a tight schedule. The Russian president is worried this may spread. We must leave now," says Alexi.

Like the good ol' days, Dr. Fraser, Alexi, and I board our old friend—the famed Soviet-era transport plane from a couple days ago. We strap down the meager supplies we brought and sit in the same seats as before, near the lone window toward the front of the cargo bay.

Staring out the ovoid window, Dr. Fraser and I say our warm goodbyes to Siberia.

"For the record, I never want to come back here. Like you could ask, 'Dr. Lawrence, would you rather eat kale for the rest of your life or go back to Siberia?' and I still think the kale would win," I say.

"I still have some kale chips left over if you want some," she says.

"No. That was like a rhetorical comparison, if those exist. I don't mean it. Kale is still overhyped and bland."

She just shrugs off my disparaging remarks, and we both continue to look out the window.

With a loud, uncomfortable sound as well as some smoke coming from all four of the engines, our plane rolls down the runway.

As the plane lifts off, Novosibirsk eventually shrinks, engulfed by the surrounding greenery.

Within no time, the behemoth of a plane defies gravity for the seventeen thousandth time, and the view from the window ceases to exist as clouds surround the plane.

Alexi climbs down from the cockpit and makes his way back into the cargo bay, stumbling over loose wires and cables on the floor.

"Okay, doctors. The flight will be quick. Only about four hours and then we should be on the ground."

I give him a thumbs up and say, "That's great. Four more hours of sleep for me," I say.

Alexi smiles and retreats back to the cockpit to speak with his Russian comrades.

"I know I've said this before, but you've been sleeping a lot lately, Lawrence. I really think something is wrong with your circadian rhythms. That might explain some of the chest pains as well," Dr. Fraser says.

"Yeah, yeah. I know. I know. Doctor Lawrence is broken, and you can fix him."

"I'm serious about this. Chest pains are no joke."

"I've been under a lot of stress lately. It's probably from the stress. I mean, you know what we've been doing, right?"

"I know. I know. It could be more serious than that," she says.

"I'm fine. Really. I am. So what? I get a little cranky, and I like to sleep a bit more."

"Okay, but I want you to get your chest pains looked at. That's not normal," she says.

Four hours later, our plane slowly descends into Moscow's airspace, touching down with the tarmac in a controlled yet violent way. Taxiing the plane for several minutes, the pilots eventually glide the aircraft into a secluded corner of the airport, far away from the international and domestic terminals.

The cargo bay door slowly opens, filling the cabin with bright rays of sunlight that temporarily blind us.

As we inch closer, we see several Russian military vehicles with flashing red and blue lights forming a blockade around the plane.

"Alexi!" I exclaim. "You didn't mention anything about a welcome party."

"I don't think it's a welcoming party," Dr Fraser adds.

Wearing gas masks and black Tychem suits, heavily armored soldiers approach the rear of the plane and shout several commands in Russian. They form a phalanx, blocking off any route of escape.

"Okay, okay," Alexi says. "They're saying that it's protocol. They want to test us to see if we are showing any symptoms of the virus."

One by one, several heavily armed Russian soldiers board the plane and begin searching through all of our belongings.

They take our temperature as well as perform a bunch of other "sensitive" tests. You get the idea—not fun.

Seeing as we are ostensibly clear of any viral infection (for now), the commander of the battalion pulls Alexi aside and explains a couple of new details as we stand off to the side in the cargo bay.

Before long, a frightened Alexi gives us the new elevator pitch.

"Okay. They have informed me that the situation is much worse than initially reported. The bad news is the patient is in a coma now, so you won't be able to talk to him at all. The good news, however, is the Russian military offered to escort us to the hospital."

Against our better judgement, we acquiesce and load our supplies into perhaps the coolest vehicle of the whole voyage: an armored personnel carrier (APC). The jet-black APC has rigid metal walls that are replete with rivets, which give it a very industrial look.

I ask Alexi if they'll let me man the gunner's seat, but they unfortunately say no.

The soldiers show us to our seats for the quick trip: a torn canvas seat that is held up by flimsy metal tubing. The whole crew eventually fits in the cramped, metal sarcophagus of the armored personnel carrier, and the roar of the tank's engines engulf the small compartment, immediately jostling us back into our seats.

"You have to admire the imagery here," I say.

"In what way?" Dr. Fraser replies.

"You know. We're sort of like Marines going into a battle we know we can't win. It's kind of sad and ominous."

"It looks that way."

CHAPTER 8:

VIREMIA

A lone red light illuminates the dark metal interior of the armored troop carrier. The rays of red light reflect on Dr. Fraser's face, revealing a tense string of emotions.

"You okay?" I ask.

"This isn't the laboratory," she says, nervously.

"Tell me about it," I say as the troop carrier slows down to a crawl, throwing us forward in our seats.

The driver shouts something in Russian and my seatmate, a heavily armored Russian man, grabs the solid metal latch and opens the door.

The sunlight rushes inside, filling every crevasse. Outside, another Russian soldier appears with an angelic halo of light around his head.

"He says we are here. He wants us to get out now," Alexi says as he extends his arm, showing the way.

In a hasty manner, we throw our bags outside on the road's concrete. Much to our dismay, the Russian soldiers do not leave our sides, bringing a whole new meaning to the term "babysitter."

"Alexi, what's the deal with comrade one and comrade two?" I ask.

"For our protection."

"What?" I say in a rather disgusted and sarcastic tone.

"They will enforce the strict protocol. This hospital is famous for being one of Russia's finest, so reputation matters a lot."

Russia's finest, he says. Russia's finest. The Central Clinical Hospital of the Presidential Administration of the Russian Federation is indeed Russia's finest. I'm not making that name up. It's a mouthful.

She looks like something out of Pripyat, Ukraine. The architecture is very, hmm . . . It's very Soviet-classical, if that makes sense. It's a giant concrete building with tiny windows, giving it an institutional feel. Although the cream-colored exterior contrasts nicely with the surrounding trees, what's on the inside is what counts. On the inside is our index case. Our patient zero, so to speak.

With our fully accoutered military escorts by our side, we casually stroll through the grandiose yet somehow plain entrance of the hospital. Through the sliding glass doors, we enter into a foyer-esque area, replete with an arcane and dilapidated carpet and fake potted plants.

"Now, where do we go?" I ask.

"Um. The signs are all in Russian, but if we can find the receptionist, then we should be able to find our index case," says Dr. Fraser.

"Doctors, please. Come this way. I will take you to the receptionist," Alexi says.

Alexi blissfully glides through the monotonous and narrow halls of the hospital like a giraffe galloping through the savanna. I know—quite the imagery.

Eventually we find our receptionist: an older blonde Russian woman sitting behind a dense sheet of plexiglass.

Through her thick plastic-framed glasses, she says, "Can I help you two?"

Her heavy Russian accent makes the translation difficult, but we manage. Dr. Fraser is, after all, a linguaphile.

"Hi. Hello. I'm Dr. Fraser, and this is Dr. Lawrence. We are from the Australian Infectious Diseases Research Centre. We have been informed that a young man from Siberia was checked into the hospital. He complained of chest pains, swelling, trouble breathing, and other problems. We would like to speak with the attending physician, please."

"Ah. You are talking about Mr. Yuri Petrov?" she says.

"I guess so," Dr. Fraser says.

"Well, Mr. Petrov went into a coma earlier today, and the attending physician has been busy with him and other patients. However, I will let her know that you are here, and she will meet you in the waiting room."

"Alright, thank you," I reply.

Dr. Fraser and I turn around and make our way into the waiting room. It's nothing lavish. The chairs are made of a wooden base with a red felt and canvas hybrid material. Eight or so chairs sit abreast, flanking the walls of the room. In the center lies a lone coffee table with Russian magazines strewn across it in every direction. Finally, the tile. Ah, the tiles give it that 1950s vibe, which most definitely complements the strange potted plant sitting in the corner covered in dust.

We sit down in the uncomfortable chairs, and Dr. Fraser says, "So, uh, I guess we wait here."

"This is how I imagined purgatory would look," I jokingly reply.

"But you're not religious," she replies.

"I dabble."

Dr. Fraser starts to nervously tap her leg on the floor, jittering like a kid who had too much sugar.

"You okay?" I ask for the second time.

"Just a little nervous," she says.

"I can tell."

"Why aren't you gnawing at your Crocs right now?" she asks.

"This isn't my first rodeo. I got infected with malaria, the *P. vivax* kind if you care, back in Africa during one of my medical assignments there, so I'm used to the pressure."

"This isn't malaria though. The symptoms are much worse."

"Well, I'm still holding out hope that it's just a heart attack, for Mr. Petrov's sake."

With time to kill until the attending physician comes, I decide to play a metaphorical game of I spy with myself. Low and behold, a lone TV graces the wall. It's not high definition, but it's enough to distract me from the potentially flesh-eating virus down the hall.

"Hey, Rebecca," I say as I tap her arm, "look on the TV. It's the World Health Organization's meeting about the virus."

"Yeah. That's Dr. Hilda Kristiansen, the head of the World Health Organization. She's the reason why we're even allowed in here. This hospital is usually heavily guarded, hence why we have comrade one and comrade two outside. I think she's Norwegian, but I'm not . . ."

"Shhhh, Rebecca. I want to hear what she has to say," I reply.

"Good evening, ladies and gentlemen," Dr. Kristiansen says. "I am going to keep this brief, as I value brevity and sincerity. About two weeks ago, we received word that a Russian ivory camp in Siberia was decimated by an unknown pathogen. We were originally under the assumption that this clandestine operation was foiled by the local police force. However, upon sending a team to the location, we now have reason to believe that a highly infectious virus is to blame. Our highly skilled team . . ."

"That's us, Rebecca. We're *apparently* highly skilled now," I butt in.

"Shhhhh," Dr. Fraser says.

"It is not a bacterium, rather it is a virus. Now, a multitude of laboratories are sequencing the genome as we speak. Because of this pathogen's unique etiology from the blood of a mammoth, we postulate it is indeed novel, with approximately only 8 percent of its genome shared among known viruses, mostly among other giant viruses. Now, this novel virus, known as a *pleistovirus* . . ."

"Wow, she used the name," I say, somberly.

"I know, I know. Now be quiet," she says.

"At the moment, we know nothing about what symptoms this virus may cause; however, we are currently tracking an initial index case in western Russia. We suspect the symptoms mirror those of known hemorrhagic fevers, because of the *pleistovirus's* hypothesized high mortality rate. Fevers, fatigue, vomiting, and nausea are to be expected. Pain particularly in the abdomen and chest are also possible. Additionally, like all known hemorrhagic fevers, this virus may cause severe internal bleeding, leading to death. The Russian government has taken proactive measures to limit the spread of this novel virus, and the WHO is currently tracking potential cases in countries such as China, Vietnam, South Korea, and Kazakhstan. However, preliminary evidence indicates this may be an isolated phenomenon, yet the World Health Organization will continue to track any potential cases. We will update you accordingly through our memos and our daily updates. Thank you." The screen cuts to black.

"China, Vietnam, and South Korea?" I say. "How many people did Yuri come into contact with?"

"I have no clue, and we won't be able to ask him either," Dr. Fraser says.

"I mean, Yuri did do a lot of 'frowned upon' things on the black market. You know, selling bones and stuff."

"If that's the case, this virus could be in Brazil for all we know," she says.

* * *

When all hope is lost, a spark of light appears: the attending physician.

Standing in the doorframe of the waiting room, she finally speaks to us: "Hello, doctors. My name is Dr. Nadia Ivanović, and I was the attending physician when Mr. Petrov entered the hospital. You have requested my service?" she says in a thick Russian accent.

"I'm Dr. Fraser, and this is Dr. Lawrence. That's Alexi, our translator."

Alexi and I give a half-hearted wave, about chest high. Nothing too fancy. We're not meeting the Queen of England.

"We're from the World Health Organization's emerging infectious disease department, and we are tasked with investigating the novel *pleistovirus* outbreak in Russia. We heard Mr. Yuri Petrov checked into the hospital today from Siberia. We believe he may be the original index case of the *pleistovirus*. Can you tell us what exactly happened when Mr. Petrov came in?" I reply.

Quick interlude: we're not from the World Health Organization, but when you're in a potential pandemic and you need things to move quickly, you do what you've got to do.

"It's tough to say because I wasn't in the waiting area, but this is what I was told. Mr. Petrov stumbled through the front door; he could barely walk. His eyes were incredibly bloodshot, like spider webs. It was very strange. Then, he started to yell. He screamed out in Russian basically asking for help because his chest hurt very bad. At first, we thought he was having a heart attack, so we took him back right away. We followed the proper protocol, giving him oxygen, nitroglycerin, and pain medicines, but nothing helped. We thought it was very weird. He's a younger gentleman, so a heart attack seemed unlikely. But you never know anymore. Then, things took a turn for the worse. He started sweating profusely; he reported trouble breathing, shortness of breath, and lots of fatigue. Stuff like that. After that, he started to violently cough. He even coughed up blood on one of the attending nurses. . . ."

"Wait, wait, wait. Did you isolate and quarantine the nurse?" I interrupt.

"Yes, yes. We did. Mr. Petrov informed us that he travelled from Siberia, and the Russian government sent out an alert a couple of days ago about travelers from Siberia. We take security very seriously here," Dr. Ivanović says.

"Alright. What other symptoms did Mr. Petrov have?" I ask.

"After he coughed up blood, we locked down the whole wing. A couple hours ago, we scrubbed down the whole emergency room wing with bleach. We put up plexiglass dividers, quarantined the receptionist, and sterilized the waiting area. After we moved him to the isolation wing, he started vomiting and reported nausea. Unfortunately, he went into a coma soon after, so we couldn't question him further. Right now, we still don't know whom he made contact with before he got to the hospital," the doctor says.

"So that's where we're at right now. He started with chest pains, which eventually led to coughing up blood and a coma. What else could the *pleistovirus* do? Has Mr. Petrov's family been alerted? What else have you done? Have you done a blood test yet? What medicine have you given him? What about X-rays and CT scans? How are the other patients feeling?" I reply.

"Okay, that's a lot of questions," Dr. Ivanović says. "After he coughed up blood and after we ruled out a heart attack, we decided to test his blood. The results were inconclusive, as we don't yet have a test for the *pleistovirus;* however, we have samples of it, and we sent them to the Vector Institute in Novosibirsk to test for antibodies. Again, we aren't entirely sure, but we decided to quarantine him just in case," Dr. Ivanović says.

"Alright, I'd like to test some of Mr. Petrov's blood myself to see if I can find anything," Dr. Fraser says.

"Of course, of course. We tried to get more information out of Mr. Petrov, but we could not get into contact with any relatives," Dr. Ivanović says.

Out of nowhere, Dr. Ivanović's beeper buzzes and startles the four of us. Upon checking the notification, she yells out in Russian to a passing staff member and quickly absconds.

"What happened? She didn't answer the rest of my questions," I add.

"Also, the World Health Organization?" Dr. Fraser says.

"I want this thing to move quickly, and I also want unrestricted access. I did what I had to do," I reply.

"Well, our unrestricted access just became restricted. Alexi, what did she say?" Dr. Fraser says.

"I couldn't hear it that well, but there was something in room number 36. I think, but I am not too sure," he says.

* * *

We rush out of the waiting room and saunter through the encapsulating halls of the hospital, trying to find Yuri in room number 36.

One by one, we check the charts outside each room, looking for Yuri Petrov's name on the manila folders. We discover some unique and odd patients being treated in this hospital: radiation poisoning, botulism, and the like. However, after a couple of minutes, we finally discover Yuri's wing, which is guarded by two more heavily armored Russian soldiers.

A makeshift poster on the door says, "Quarantine Wing: masks and PPE required."

Wasting no time, we don our spare personal protective equipment: N95 masks, gloves, face shields, and our trusty white Tychem suits.

However, the Russian soldiers forming a phalanx outside of the quarantine wing do not budge. They hold firm, not even acknowledging our existence.

After much tribulation and persuasion, we eventually get access after Alexi informs them of our clout in the infectious disease world.

Stepping through the narrow doors is like stepping into a war zone.

* * *

Although there's no gunfire, the situation is equally scary. We could potentially have the next Ebola or COVID-19 on our hands, and we don't even know it yet. That's the world of emerging infectious diseases though: it's complicated, like the immune system itself.

Without knowing the genome of the *pleistovirus,* creating a vaccine will be hard and time consuming. Most vaccines take years to develop, unless you have the power of every industrialized nation in the world working toward that common goal. For the time being, it's impossible.

Unfortunately in Yuri's case, the rudimentary prophylactics the team administered weren't enough to stop the virus. Viruses are strange, and universal treatment options like remdesivir won't work for every virus.

Upon entering the wing, we immediately see Dr. Ivanović sloped against the glass wall of Yuri's room in a depressed state.

We quickly walk over to offer our emotional support.

In a somber tone, Dr. Fraser says, "Nadia, it will be alright. Your team did everything they could. You followed the protocol exactly. There's nothing more you could've done. Yuri fought for as long as he could."

"I'll be fine. I wouldn't worry about me; I would check up on Dr. Lawrence. He looks pretty shaken up," Dr. Ivanović says.

"Lawrence, are you okay?" Dr. Fraser asks.

"Yeah, yeah. Never better." I wipe my hand across my eyes to clear away the tears. "That could've been me when I got malaria. Before this expedition, I never called my parents to thank them and say my goodbyes, in case you know."

"Don't think like that. You'll be fine. You haven't been exposed to it yet," she says.

"We don't know that. The incubation period of this virus is up in the air right now. The top end is two weeks, but we don't know what kind of viral load Mr. Petrov was exposed to. The incubation period could be as short as a day or two. We don't know yet. We need more data," I reply.

"If it calms your fears, we can test your blood if you would like," Dr. Ivanović says.

"Great. More needles," I say.

"We'll have Lawrence test his blood later, and we'll test mine as well, just to be safe. For now, what's changed considering the recent developments?" Dr. Fraser asks.

"Alright, so here's what we know now. It has a high mortality rate with one confirmed infection and one confirmed death. We didn't find any other bodies at the camp, so that rules out any other confirmed cases and deaths. It's probably viremic, meaning in the blood. Method of transmission is still up in the air. Right now, it's most likely spread through direct contact with an infected patient and direct contact with blood. We'll need to schedule an autopsy in order to confirm if it is viremia, but if I were a betting man, I'd say it is," I reply.

"Agreed. I'll have my team perform an autopsy as soon as possible," Dr. Ivanović says.

"Now, without seeing what the virus did to Yuri's internal organs, it's hard to tell which ones are affected. In my opinion, I think it's most likely hemorrhagic. Nothing kills this quick, so it must take a toll on the insides. That means it most likely attacks several organs at once in several different locations. That way, it can overrun the immune system, killing faster. Do we know how long Yuri was experiencing his chest pains?

That may tell us when the virus started replicating profusely,"
I ask.

"Not really; we asked several times, but he kept giving us
different answers. At first, he said a day or so, but then he
revised it to three and four days. The last time we asked him,
he said a week," Dr. Ivanović says.

"Okay, so it's either a day or a week. Perfect. Misinformation
is really something special. Alright, plan B: the coma. The
coma doesn't help. It just jumbles the whole thing. Well . . ."

"Well . . . what?" Dr. Fraser says.

"I mean. It's a possibility. A wild one, but it's a possibility
right now."

"Brevity, Lawrence. We're on a schedule here," Dr. Fraser says.

"Comas are caused by a variety of things. Usually, it's
a traumatic brain injury or tumors— among other things.
However, comas can also be caused by a stroke, a lack of
blood going to the brain. Now, this lack of blood could be
caused by a variety of things: a bunch of diseases, diabetes, or
blood clots. Given the present information—hear me out—I
think our little *pleistovirus* causes an excessive amount of
blood clots, some of which break off called embolisms. However, I *need* the autopsy results to confirm all of that. Right
now, it's just pure speculation. A hypothesis. A gamble. You
get the idea," I say.[37]

"Yes. I will go and schedule it for today. Please excuse me,"
Dr. Ivanović says.

Dr. Ivanović shuffles through the wide corridors of the
hospital out of our view.

---

37   Samantha Harrington, "How Climate Change Affects Mental
Health," *Yale Climate Connections*, February 4, 2020.

"Alright, now that my work is done for today, I need to take a nap," I say.

"Wait, wait, wait. Not so fast, Lawrence. While we await the autopsy results, you promised me you'd see a doctor about your chest pains," Dr. Fraser inquires.

"Urgh. I thought you were joking about that."

"Well, I'm not."

"Alright, so whom you do recommend? Do you have anybody in mind? I want one that really catches my vibe. You know?"

"No, I don't have one in mind, but I can find one. Give me a minute. I'll go make some calls," she says.

She leaves me standing there in the hall, alone next to a gurney.

While I'm there, nurses shuffle in and out of Mr. Petrov's room. Within a half hour of his death, his room is already cleaned. The nurses do, however, take their time. They are thorough. They strip the bed, replacing it with clean, sterile sheets. They disinfect every surface: the tables, the floors, and even the windows. Finally, they bag up the trash and tie it in disposable, red biohazard bags, which are headed for the incinerator. As quickly as Mr. Petrov arrived, he is gone.

* * *

Deep in thought about what might lie ahead, I serendipitously receive a text message from Dr. Fraser: "Hey, found a cardiologist. He says he knows you. Meet in room 15 on the X wing."

I guess I'm an infamous man, even in Russia. Hopefully, he wasn't one of my old lab partners. If that's the case, I have some explaining to do.

I retrace my steps through the hospital, going back into the main hall and reorienting myself. Under the fluorescent lights, the interior is rather drab. I know I've probably already mentioned this, but the walls have an expired cream-like color to them. To make matters worse, all of the signage is in Russian. Luckily, thanks to my days during college playing a video game popular is Russia, I know a thing or two about the language.

* * *

I eventually stumble upon the empty room number 15 with a lone gurney flanking one wall. The room is cozy and well lit with windows letting in ample quantities of light. There's a singular chair in the corner and a lone windowpane.

Like an inquisitive houseguest, I plop myself down on the hospital bed and stare blankly at the popcorn-style ceiling.

"Knock, knock. Am I interrupting Dr. Lawrence's special time?" Dr. Fraser says.

"Very funny. I'm glad I taught you a thing or two about comedy."

"I learned everything from books, not you," she says.

"This is the real world, sweetheart. Books can't predict everything."

Out of the corner of my eye, a third person enters the room, and to my surprise, I do indeed know him.

"Oh my god, if it isn't Richard Peterson," I say.

"Um. There should be a 'Dr.' in front of that. How's it going Lawrence? Long time no see," Dr. Peterson replies.

"My bad, doctor. It's alright. It's been far too long. What've you been up to?"

"I'm sorry, what's the connection here? Were you two like roommates in college?" Dr. Fraser says.

"Ah. Dr. Fraser, this is Dr. Peterson. We worked in West Africa for a little while. Mostly doing research. We studied the effects of malaria on heart failure. It was really interesting stuff."

"I'm hoping you didn't let Dr. Lawrence take blood samples. The man couldn't use a needle to save his life," Dr. Peterson says.

"That's the Lawrence that I know. Hasn't changed a bit," Dr. Fraser says.

"Alright, so Dr. Lawrence, Dr. Fraser tells me that you have a couple of problems. Tell me about them," he says as he sits down in the lone chair.

"Oh boy. We're really doing this? Okay. I mean if it's what Dr. Fraser wants, then I'll do it. Where do I begin? Well, as you may know, I've been in the Siberian wilderness for the past couple of days, researching a new, potentially deadly virus. So, I guess you could say that I haven't been getting enough sleep. . . ."

"Technically, you've been getting more than enough sleep, like twelve and thirteen hours," Dr. Fraser interjects.

"Fine, so I have been sleeping a lot lately; however, it hasn't really helped. I still have bloodshot eyes; I'm tired all the time, and my chest hurts."

"Talk to me about your chest for a minute. Where exactly does it hurt?" Dr. Peterson asks.

"Here. Here. Here. Here." I point all over. "It's just a mild pain, nothing too serious though." I add.

"Interesting. I'd like to run some diagnostic tests, but I don't think it's too serious. I would also like to take some blood tests. That would allow me to narrow down the list of possible things."

"It could be all psychological," I reply.

"In what way?" Dr. Peterson asks.

"You know, like seasonal affective disorder."

"I'm not a psychiatrist or a psychologist, but it's a far-out possibility."

"It's not far out."

"What has your appetite been like since you left for Siberia?" Dr. Peterson says.

"I've been pretty healthy. Lots of kale, avocados, the occasional whole tuna. You know, normal stuff," I reply.

"Dr. Peterson, he ate an entire box of Tim Tams and brought a caseload of barbecue sauce into the tundra," Dr. Fraser says.

"Okay, somebody is craving carbohydrates, and you're still obsessed with barbecue sauce?" Dr. Peterson asks.

"Born and raised in the South," I reply. "There is something else that could be causing my chest problems," I add.

"What's that?"

"Ever since Mike and Ike split, I've never been the same," I reply.

"Doctors really do make the worst patients," Dr. Peterson says.

"Do you know what's sad, Dr. Peterson?"

"What?" he replies.

"It's not about cardiology, so humor me for a second," I reply. "This whole seasonal affective disorder thing is actually only going to get worse as time goes on."

"What do you mean?" he asks.

"Yeah, Lawrence. What do you mean?" Dr. Fraser asks.

"Climate change," I reply.

"Don't worry about it, Dr. Peterson. Lawrence has been peddling this theory since we arrived in Siberia," Dr. Fraser says.

"No, no. I'm serious. As the climate continues to change, more extreme and deadlier weather events may become commonplace. These events—hurricanes, monsoons, droughts, all of it—may cause physical and mental trauma, including anxiety, depression, post-traumatic stress disorder, and maybe even chest pains. Am I wrong?" I ask.[38]

"Technically, no to the chest pains part. . . ." Dr. Peterson says.

"Doesn't matter. I'm proving a point." I conclude.

"Well, Lawrence. Those are, uh, interesting hypotheses, but for you, I recommend getting some rest. Your blood work should come back soon," Dr. Peterson says.

"See ya later, Lawrence. Get some good rest." Dr. Fraser says.

---

38   Anne-Marie Connolly-Andersen, Heather Whitaker, Jonas Klingström, and Clas Ahlm, "Risk of Venous Thromboembolism Following Hemorrhagic Fever With Renal Syndrome: A Self-Controlled Case Series Study," *Clinical Infectious Diseases* 66, no. 2 (January 2018): 268-273.

CHAPTER 9

INCUBATION

I wake up in a chaotic environment. My blanket and pillows are strewn across the floor in a wayward pattern, signaling a struggle took place in the night. I was fighting against my body. I did not win.

Around midnight, my body's natural ways of maintaining homeostasis went awry, and I started sweating profusely. After my blanket became drenched in sweat, presumably because of the incredibly humid hospital air, I decided to eject them onto the floor. Then, a couple of hours later, around 3 a.m., my body's chest kicked it into overdrive, producing an incredible pain. I'm not sure what is was, but I am very concerned. A chest pain for someone in their thirties is never, ever a good sign.

As I sit up on my gurney, I start to run through hypothetical scenarios in my head like any normal person would.

I've had a kidney stone before, and although it hurt like hell, it was in my lower abdomen, not my upper body near my heart. That facet scratches that off. Could it be a heart attack? Again, I'm fairly young and fairly healthy, so no, probably not. I know, I know. I do have an obsession with carbohydrate-laden foods, but I eat them in moderation. It's fine.

I run through a full laundry list of ideas until it hits me. The pain becomes unbearable, causing me to curl up on the bed. In the fetal position with a pillow by my side, I hear a knock at the door.

"Oh boy, what's wrong?" asks Dr. Fraser in a concerned tone.

"Incredible chest pains. Sweating profusely. Fever. Fatigue. My whole body aches," I reply.

"Oh my," Dr. Fraser says as her mouth drops. "I'll call the attending physician and see if they can administer something to fight the pain. Do you know what it is?"

"Not really. Ow. Ow. Ow. It feels like an alien making its way through my veins."

"You didn't lose your sense of imagination, I see."

I give a faint smile and cry out in pain. "Dear Lord! It hurts."

"Do you think it's a kidney stone? My aunt had one, and she looked, more or less, like you do now."

"Probably not," I say as I clutch my chest. "See if you can schedule me a CT scan. . . . Owwwwww. . . . It's worth a shot."

"Alright, I'll see if I can schedule you one. If it is a kidney stone, the CT scan should pick it up," she says as she nervously bites her fingernails. "Your blood tests should be done by today as well, so that should give us some indication as well. . . ."

A loud jingle envelops the whole room, and Dr. Fraser looks at me.

"Is that your phone?" she asks.

"Not mine. Mine's dead. It's yours."

Dr. Fraser sifts through her black leather purse until she finally finds it.

"Hello?" Dr. Fraser says. "Ah, yes. Dr. Ivanović, how is it going?" she continues.

Although I can't hear what they're saying, I see Dr. Fraser's facial expressions changing; her eyebrows raise; and her mouth gapes open. Then, she lets out an audible sigh as she rests her face in her palm and says: "Thanks for letting me know." She hangs up the phone.

"What? What did she say?" I inquire.

She grabs the empty seat near the front door of the room and hangs her head in her hands.

"My test results?" I inquire. "Is it bad?"

With tears running down her face, she nods her head.

"How bad is it? Is it a malarial relapse? Is that what it is?"

In a somber tone, she says, "I'm sorry, Lawrence. This is all my fault. I should've been a better boss. We should've followed . . ."

"What? It's not the malaria."

"No, uh, it's . . . um . . . it's the *pleistovirus.* They found it in your blood stream, and it's all my fault."

With pain radiating throughout my body, I gingerly reply: "Rebecca, it's not your fault," as tears start to form in my eyes. "For all we know, it could be a false positive. I was never exposed to it. You handled all of the sampling. Remember?"

"Lawrence, there could've been a micro-abrasion on your suit from the sharp rocks of the cave. Infected blood spewed all over us." She starts to rub her eyes. "I should've had us wear the aprons and extra protective equipment."

I painstakingly realign myself in order to face her and say, "Nobody could've predicted this."

The beads of sweat continue to drip down my forehead, merging with the tears and snot dripping down my nose.

"If anything, we know it isn't a respiratory virus."

"How do you know that?" she asks.

With my hand clenching my heart, I say, "Because you haven't become infected. It's probably a nonaerosolized hemorrhagic fever of some kind. If it's like Ebola, it spreads through direct contact with body fluids like blood."

Dr. Fraser's expression turns blank, and she stops crying for a second. Then, she stares blankly and says: "Lawrence, that's far worse."

"I know, but it's not pandemic-level bad. Go make some calls to Dr. Lancaster and get me a CT scan so we can know for sure. The pain is getting worse."

"I'll let you make a couple of phone calls while I go trace down Dr. Ivanović and the rest of the staff. I'll be back soon. Don't go anywhere."

"Couldn't even move if I wanted to," I reply.

She absconds, leaving me alone in a room with just my thoughts.

Now, I'm not going to bore you with the poignant details concerning my phone call with my parents. I'm estranged from them, so needless to say, they weren't expecting a call in the middle of the night. I haven't talked to them in a year, so it was a nice refresher to hear their voices. I wish it was under different circumstances, but . . .

* * *

Normally, I would be all jovial to have an index case on my hands, but I'm not used to being the guinea pig.

Dr. Ivanović eventually spoils the serenity, giving me a meager dose of morphine to quell any pain, and to my surprise, it helps a little. She and her team of about two other people surround me. Dressed in a full array of personal protective equipment, they start taking my vitals.

"Temperature 102.4 degrees," one nurse calls out.

Another nurse calls out something about my blood pressure being low.

Then, Dr. Ivanović says, "Dr. Fraser has requested that you undergo a CT scan to, hopefully, clear up a confusion. However, the preliminary blood diagnostic reveals that you have the *pleistovirus* in your blood, and we were able to detect trace amounts of antibodies against it, which is a very good sign."

"Good. I want you to use my antibodies for research. Dr. Ivanović, figure out what this thing does to humans." I cry out in pain, clenching my chest again. "Oh, also, if I do end up passing, give this letter to Dr. Fraser." I hand her a small, white envelope.

"I can do that. Anything you need," she says.

Dr. Ivanović and her team wheel my gurney out into the empty halls. A couple hours ago, these halls were filled with patients and doctors. Now, it's a ghost town.

As I lie back in the bed, the bright, white LED lights shine in my eyes, giving me flashbacks to when I was hospitalized with malaria. That story, however, ended on a brighter note. . . .

The gurney abruptly turns and accelerates through two large double doors with a sign that says "Radiology" written in English and Russian.

After a five-minute ride, the bed eventually decelerates, placing me directly outside of the CT scan room, or computerized tomography room for the nerds.

The severity of the situation finally hits me as I am wheeled through the doors and see the radiologist wearing head-to-toe PPE. This thing is serious.

The tall man steps out of his office and maintains a six-foot distance from me, saying: "Hello, Dr. Lawrence. My name is Dr. Boris Orlov, and I'll be conducting your CT scan today."

"I'd give you a heartier welcome, but my insides are killing me," I reply.

"That's okay. It's okay. Now, even though you may be familiar with CT scans, I'm required to brief all of my patients before we begin. Is that okay?"

"Yeah, sure. I really don't have anywhere to go," I say in agony.

"Perfect. A CT scan, if you don't already know, stands for a computerized tomography scan. It's basically a more advanced X-ray system. Normally, X-rays only produce a single two-dimensional image; however, a CT scan can produce a three-dimensional image using multiple X-ray images. Here, follow me, I'll show you the different parts of the machine," he says.[39]

"Here it is. This is the CT scan machine. Now, the dough-nut-shaped end of the machine is called the gantry, and it's where all of the sensitive X-ray equipment is," he says.

I slouch over in the gurney, compacting my chest to relieve the pain.

"This end is the motorized table aspect of the machine. This is where you will lie down and the table will gently slide into the gantry, allowing us to get a visual of what's going on."

Normally, I'd cut Boris off because of my excruciating pain; however, I decide to let him finish because the mor-phine that one of the nurses administered is starting to kick in, giving me a few brief moments sans any pain.

---

39   "Radiation-Emitting Products: Computed Tomography (CT)," U.S. Food and Drug Administration, Last Modified June 14, 2019.

"So, when the table slides into the gantry, the X-ray sensors in the tubular doughnut will start to rotate around you. Every complete rotation yields a two-dimensional image, or slice, of your body. When it's over, we will have multiple images, or slices, of your body. Think of it like bread. Do you like bread?" he asks.

"I mean, bread is alright," I say with a tilted head and a raised eyebrow.

I guess what they say about radiologists is true: they're very socially awkward. Boris most definitely sits in a dark room all day staring at screens. It beats getting infected with a virus, so he wins.

"Well, an X-ray is like a single slice of bread; whereas, the CT scan is like a whole loaf of bread. Which would you rather have?"

"How hungry am I?" I inquire.

"You can't make a sandwich with one slice of bread. Therefore, a CT scan is better because we can use a single slice or we can use the whole loaf to get a three-dimensional view of all of your organs," he replies.

"Moving on, the CT scanner will emit several radiation beams that will penetrate your body. These beams will pass through your body, and detectors will read them. Once picked up, the data will transmit to our computers, and a three-dimensional tomographic image of your body will be produced."

"I don't mean to rush things, but can we get things rolling yet?" I ask.

"Unfortunately, not yet. Because we are dealing with soft tissues, such as your blood vessels, we will need to inject you with a contrast agent. CT machines are notorious for not picking up soft tissues like veins and blood vessels. They are much more reliable for picking up bones. However, the contrast agent, like iodine in our case, will allow us to visualize your blood vessels and see the effects on the circulatory system. We'll put you on an IV and inject the contrast agent into your blood vessels while you're in the machine to maximize efficiency," Dr. Orlov says.[40]

"Good ahead. Inject more stuff," I say as I start to become dizzy.

Dr. Orlov retreats back to his office and his nurse follows through with his orders: politely telling me to undress.

A bit much, you might ask, but he assured me that any metal will interfere with the sensitive acoustic machinery.

With the gracefulness of a young goat, I gingerly undress down to my underwear and don a disposable hospital gown. Most of the chest pain has subsided with the introduction of the morphine, leaving me in a more upbeat mentality. However, I'm still sweating bullets, I still have a raging fever, and I'm feeling incredibly dizzy.

"Alright, nurse, I'm done," I yell out.

"Okay, perfect. Follow me."

After almost falling on the floor, I finally scale the meter-high CT scan, lying down on the gantry.

After the nurse attaches an IV, he too absconds, leaving me in a room all by myself.

That's when things start to fall apart for me.

The motorized table of the CT machine gently inches forward at a snail's pace with me lying on the bed.

The gantry feels cold and metallic. The sweat dripping down from my chest forms a puddle near my back, providing

---

40   "Computed Tomography (CT)," National Institute of Biomedical Imaging and Bioengineering, Date Accessed October 11, 2020.

a brief cooling sensation. Then, the sensitive X-ray equipment powers up. It makes a loud and irritating sound. It beeps and buzzes. It sounds like a glorified microwave that's frying my insides.

Over the intercom, I hear Dr. Orlov giving me information in a mechanical sounding voice.

"Okay, Lawrence. Don't mind the sounds. The sounds only mean that the machine is working. Not much longer, maybe fifteen more minutes."

Dr. Fraser enters into the other room and begins talking with the radiologist.

"Hello, Dr. Orlov. I'm Dr. Fraser, one of Dr. Lawrence's acquaintances."

"Nice to meet you. He is getting his CT scans now. We should be getting our first images shortly."

The obnoxious drone of the CT machine puts me into a weary state. To make matters worse, my pain switches away from my chest and migrates to my muscles and bones. The pain is inexplicable. All you have to know is that it's worse than getting kicked in the . . .

My eyes start to flutter, and I start to zone out, slipping in and out of consciousness.

In the other room, Dr. Orlov receives the first of several hundred images on his computer screen.

"Okay, let's see what we're dealing with here," he says as he scrolls through the files on his desktop.

"Well, there's one blood clot in his arm. It looks like a hemorrhage. Maybe he came into contact with a viral hemorrhagic fever or something like that," he says.

"Really? I guess Lawrence was right. One blood clot is not terrible though. Right?" Dr. Fraser says.

"Not necessarily. It can be pretty bad," he says. "Usually blood clots, which lead to hemorrhages, start out when the blood vessel is broken. The *pleistovirus* may have something to do with this aspect. Then, platelets, which are floating around in the blood vessels, are activated by signaling cells. These platelets will form a makeshift plug on the broken endothelium, which is the blood vessel's cell wall, and it will stop blood from leaking out of the blood vessel."[41]

If I were in the room and in a better state, I would most likely make a joke about platelets being the Flex Seal of the body, but alas.

"When the platelets settle in, they send out signals to more platelets and other cells and so forth. Again, our *pleistovirus* may have something to do with the signaling of the platelets. It may permanently 'turn them on,' so to speak, such that a clot forms regardless of if there's a breakage of the blood vessel. Clotting can also form another way: through thromboplastin. The disintegration of the platelets releases an enzyme, called thromboplastin. The *pleistovirus* may cause the unnecessary degradation of platelets in the blood, leading to a higher concentration of thromboplastin. Thromboplastin will then convert prothrombin, a normal protein found in the blood, into thrombin. Continuing down the line, thrombin will eventually convert fibrinogen, another protein in the blood, into fibrin. This fibrin forms a netlike structure around the broken blood vessel, which traps blood cells and leads to the clot. Unfortunately, without knowing

---

41   Corey Binns, "New Insight into How Blood Clots," *LiveScience,* November 6, 2006.

which method of clotting is activated, treatment is going to be hard," he says.[42]

"I know. That's why we needed to study our index case," Dr. Fraser says.

Dr. Fraser begins pacing around the room with her hand rested against her chin.

"So what do the other images show?" she asks.

"Um, let's see. Here's an image of his other arm." Dr. Orlov points to the computer screen." He has two more clots in his left arm. Dr. Fraser, I have never seen anything like this in the arms. Clots are mostly in the legs, not usually in the arms."

"Well, can you fix it?" she says.

"The arms, most likely. The good news is that we caught them fast, and it's only in the arms right now," he says.

Several more minutes go by and the machine continues to whirl away, taking tomographic slices of my internal organs.

* * *

Eventually the final chest scans are downloaded, and Dr. Orlov begins to diagnose my condition.

"Alright, let's see what the chest scans have to show. . . . Oh, lord."

"Wait. What? What's wrong?" she says.

"Look. Here, here, here . . . here, here, and here," he says. "All those places are complete blood clots, and here, here, and here are blood clots that are in the beginning phases of formation. There's far too many for us to treat. We could

---

42   Rustem I. Litvinov and John W. Weisel, "What Is the Biological and Clinical Relevance of Fibrin?" *Seminars in Thrombosis and Hemostasis* 42, no. 4 (June 2016).

try and operate, but the disease will most likely outpace us. Dr. Lawrence will be dead before the procedure is over. His conditions are deteriorating as we speak. Yuri's scans were almost identical: there were fifteen, if not more, blood clots all throughout his body, some of which broke off and led to a stroke," he says.

As time progresses, I begin to experience a shortness of breath and I violently gasp for air. With a lack of oxygen reaching my brain, my body begins to shut down, and I black out. Everything turns into a blur. The virus takes over my body and I enter into a coma, much like Yuri did.

"Shit. Nurse! Nurse! Come here!" Dr. Orlov exclaims as he waves his hand. "Help me get Dr. Lawrence into another room; he's gone into a coma. Dr. Fraser, call Dr. Ivanović now and tell her to get here as fast as possible." he says.

The virus debilitates me quickly. Blood clots form via an unknown method, and my body slowly starts to shut down as oxygen is not delivered to my organs.

Dr. Orlov and the nurses dexterously load me back on the gurney and transport me to the nearest room. When we enter the room, the hospital staff try everything in their power to keep me alive, but I've already entered into a coma-like state.

Time slows down.

It's too late.

CHAPTER 10:

EPILOGUE

———

Several hours pass and the hospital becomes a ghost town. The staff as well as the patients were evacuated when I took a turn for the worse.

The sound of silence eventually engulfs the halls as my coma eventually stabilizes. My vitals begin to hover around Yuri's previously recorded averages, which is still very concerning. Unfortunately, the situation does not bode well as my blood continues to clot, virtually squeezing the life out of me.

It's only a matter of time until my coma, like Yuri's, turns fatal.

Dr. Fraser hasn't left the room since the nurses initially transferred me. Even against the advice of the nurses, Dr. Fraser stayed. Seated in the lone chair next to the door, she decides to call Dr. Lancaster to update him on my feeble condition. Dr. Lancaster informs her that he's already en route to Moscow in order to provide support in any way he can. Unfortunately, he does inform her that my death is imminent, which doesn't sit well with her.

The distraught and frazzled Dr. Fraser hangs up the phone and anxiously gazes upon my face. She's hoping for a sign of life, but she won't get one.

Dr. Ivanović enters the cuboid, white-walled room, still wearing her full regalia of PPE.

"Dr. Fraser, before Lawrence's condition deteriorated a couple of hours ago, he gave me this."

Dr. Ivanović hands Dr. Fraser my letter and a lone banana from the hospital's cafeteria.

Upon witnessing the slightly bruised banana, Dr. Fraser begins to grin and say: "Oh, Dr. Lawrence. You shouldn't have."

"I'll give you some time alone. Dr. Lawrence's condition will continue to deteriorate, and he will most likely succumb as Yuri did. However, we're currently in contact with experts from around the world, addressing every option."

With a half-hearted smile, Dr. Fraser nods her head and returns to her chair.

She haphazardly tears through the envelope as she begins to eat the banana.

Dear Rebecca, I told you that I'd pay you back someday. You wouldn't believe the strings I had to pull to get that banana, so please, cherish it. Don't eat it right away.

Rebecca immediately says, "Whoops." She turns to me in my coma-like state and says, "My bad, Lawrence."

These past few weeks have been incredible. I've learned some new things, I had some laughs, and I've even managed to teach an old dog some new tricks. No offense. You've given me a new perspective on life, and I want to thank you by sharing mine. Life's too short—trust me on this one. We have a finite amount

of time on this earth, and we shouldn't squander it by being angry, depressed, or sad. Every day, I woke up with the same motto: I wanted to put a smile on someone's face. Life is tough, but comedy heals almost all wounds (I don't think comedy can fix a blood clot. Just saying). So, you may have found my behavior a bit, say, erratic or strange, but I can assure you it was a product of my past and it has a purpose. I moved around quite a bit—different schools, cities, states. Because of this, I was never able to "settle down" and have a normal life. However, comedy was a way for me to live my life stress free in a chaotic environment. I guess what I'm trying to say is this: you may think I'm a total goofball, but I can assure you my brain works just fine.
XOXO,
Dr. Lawrence.

Tears begin to roll down her cheeks as she says, "You're still a goofball to me."

Located near the fake potted plant in the corner, the TV begins broadcasting an emergency press conference from the World Health Organization.

"Hello, ladies and gentlemen. My name is Dr. Kristiansen, the head of the World Health Organization. In the past twenty-four hours, the situation concerning the novel *pleistovirus* has changed. We are currently monitoring a case in Russia's capital and one potential case in Beijing. We were able to obtain antibodies from the blood of the infected individuals, which we will research to test their efficacy. These antibodies, if they are deemed effective, will be used to make lifesaving medications should the *pleistovirus* spread internationally.

"Additionally, with the help of labs in Australia, the United States, Belgium, and Egypt, we were able to trace the entire genome of the *pleistovirus*, and we are working on developing a rapid diagnostic test. This test will ensure the rapid identification of any *pleistovirus* infections, allowing us to quickly contain any initial outbreak. Although no new cases have arisen in the past twenty-four hours, the Russian and Chinese governments continue to perform contract tracing for any individuals who have travelled from Siberia. These methods have proven indispensable as one potential case has been isolated in Beijing, China. At the moment, the individual is currently quarantined and is receiving antivirals such as remdesivir to treat this novel hemorrhagic fever. Because no formal, proven vaccine currently exists for the *pleistovirus*, we advise the upmost caution when traveling internationally, especially to Siberia. Like all emerging epidemics, this situation is rapidly evolving, so we advise you to consult the World Health Organization's website for up-to-date information. Thank you. Are there any questions?"

A NOTE FROM THE AUTHOR

Everything in life is unexpected.

When I was a child, my father, a mellow man who frequently regaled me with advice, told me I should "always plan for variable change." As a young middle school student, I did not really know what he meant, and for the most part I carried on living my normal life, watching the *Discovery Channel* and *Animal Planet* for hours on end. I didn't know it at the time, but my true passion was and still is science. As the years progressed, I became more well versed in scientific literature and programs. I was fascinated with the mysteries of the natural world these programs and books explored. From pathogens to penguins, I was hooked. To me, the idea that a nonliving, microscopic virus could debilitate a human was incredibly frightening yet alluring, and it sparked a lifelong voyage of curiosity. By the same token, Steve Irwin, my childhood hero, taught me to respect nature and the environment, which has fundamentally altered my lifestyle. Steve gave me a green thumb: I became aware of human and animal interactions, I began to respect mother nature and all of her power, and I began to see the connection between the environment and global health.

However, as I started reading more scientific literature in high school, I realized our environment is changing and old viruses are reemerging. I knew I wanted to help in any way that I could. Unfortunately, I was still a young teenager, so my options were limited. I spent hours reading books and watching educational documentaries, which laid the foundation for my thinking about the natural world. By watching these scientific-oriented programs at an early age, I learned how climate change and medicine are interconnected. Now, as a sophomore in college, I am poised to join the next generation of scientists who are tasked with tackling the new challenges in medicine posed by climate change.

The public is, sadly, grossly misinformed about climate change. The climate is indeed changing. According to NASA, earth's average surface temperature has risen nearly 1.62 degrees Fahrenheit, enough to cause a lasting impact on many ecosystems. This global rise in temperature will undoubtedly lead to clear and concrete consequences, such as rising tides, more snowmelt, and melting ice caps. However, this is where many proponents of climate change action stop. These proponents advocate palliative policies that merely relieve the first-order consequences of climate change. By adopting such a narrow-minded view, we endanger a large subset of the world's population who will suffer from loosely studied and poorly understood second-order consequences.

These second order consequences are potentially wide ranging, encompassing physical health as well as mental health. In a future with a disrupted climate, we may see incidences of climate refugees suffering from PTSD, we may see a resurgence of seasonal affective disorder (SAD), or we may see an entirely new disorder develop. As the climate shifts, new mental health ailments may become more prevalent, and billions, if not millions, will be put in peril, stretching our underfunded health care system too thin. Unfortunately, the public has turned a blind eye to these potentially catastrophic second-order consequences. Additionally, with budget cuts proposed, around $85 million in proposed cuts to the Centers for Disease Control's Emerging and Zoonotic Infectious Diseases Department, these second-order consequences may never be understood. Thus, they are purely speculation for the time being. However, one thing remains constant: climate change will affect everyone no matter your geographic location, and as a result we all have a part to play in stopping it.[43]

In regard to physical health, the connection is clear cut. For instance, the most recent COVID-19 pandemic, as well as most epidemics, stems from a centuries-long battle with nature. Humans, with a lust for development, have inexplicably altered the environment, pushing closer into the deep unknown. As humans continue to expand the wildland-urban interface, deforesting lands once pristine, we come into direct contact with potential vectors such as mosquitoes and bats among others. By settling in these once-remote parts of the world, humans absolutely increase their risk of infection—mosquito bites may become more common because of overgrowth and an abundance of water; with a lack of suitable trees, bats will nest inside homes, increasing the risk of contact; humans may be exposed to a new pathogen

---

43   U.S. Department of Health and Human Services, *"Justification of Estimates for Appropriation Committees,"* Washington, DC, 2020, Date Accessed September 15, 2020.

that was tucked away in the deep depths of the previously untouched forest.

Regardless of the vector, these new and old pathogens deserve our full attention in the twenty-first century. As Earth's population continues to climb toward eight billion people, the risk of a potential pandemic increases. An additional problem that deserves our attention stems from the environment itself. As global temperatures continue to rise, permafrost around the world will undoubtedly melt, which may release a treasure trove of novel viruses and bacteria into the modern world. Attempts to use our modern antibiotics and vaccines may prove fruitless, and as a result we must prepare for the inevitable consequences. Either scenario produces consequences that we are regrettably familiar with: millions, potentially billions, of infections and a substantial loss of life.

Although the challenge of climate change may be daunting, there is a clear path to success: we need more young adults in science, technology, engineering, and mathematics, or STEM for short. There was a time in my life where I had almost given up my STEM endeavors. However, after reading *The Martian* as a freshman in high school, my passion was reignited. In fact, *The Martian* even spurred me to teach two summer courses focused on science, technology, and the environment as well as one on interstellar space travel. Not only did I deepen my appreciation for academia, but I also learned the importance of stories. Because the majority of my students were in middle school, I had to alter my pedagogy in order to involve movies, books, and stories. That's when I learned the power a book can have. By having my class read parts of *The Martian*, I was able to gain their attention while also teaching them about the intricacies of a Martian colony. *The Martian* served as a springboard for my students and me into the important field of STEM, and as a result it managed to inspire several young scientists. In writing my book, *Etiology*, I wasn't trying to start a movement. I merely wanted to pique every young adult's interest in the connection between medicine and climate change. Through the lens of a young infectious disease doctor named Dr. Lawrence, the reader will embark on a journey throughout the world looking for the next "big" pathogen. Although the story is told through a science fiction lens, it incorporates relevant scientific procedures and knowledge as well as a little bit of humor.

In 2020, with the COVID-19 pandemic sweeping every nation, the connection between the environment and public health has never been stronger. Thirty-seven million people have been infected and millions more have been inversely affected; although one thing remains constant: our lives have changed forever. In the future, these anomalies may become commonplace and the loss of life may inch into the billions. As a result, in order to preemptively target the next pandemic and to tackle emerging infectious diseases, we need more students studying STEM. For now, I hope this book will light a spark in the next generation. Although at the moment all we can do is expect the unexpected.[44]

---

44 Johns Hopkins University of Medicine, "COVID-19 Dashboard by the Center For Systems Science and Engineering (CSSE) At Johns Hopkins University (JHU)," Date Last Modified October 11, 2020.

ACKNOWLEDGMENTS

This book would not be possible without the help of two of my esteemed professors: professor Cynthia Wei of Georgetown University and professor Kasey Christopher of Duquesne University. Throughout this whole process, they routinely regaled me with their wisdom and knowledge, teaching me everything I know about the environment and biology. Additionally, I would also like to acknowledge my friends who sacrificed their precious time to beta read my book. Lastly, I would like to acknowledge two important sources of inspiration: David Quammen (the author of *Spillover: Animal Infections and the Next Human Pandemic*) and C.J. Peters (the author of *Virus Hunter: Thirty Years of Battling Hot Viruses Around the World*).

Thank you for everything!
You made this book possible.

APPENDIX

CHAPTER 1

National Human Genome Research Institute. "Deoxyribonucleic Acid (DNA) Fact Sheet." Date Last Modified August 24, 2020. https://www.genome.gov/about-genomics/fact-sheets/Deoxyribonucleic-Acid-Fact-Sheet

National Human Genome Research Institute. "Histone." Date Accessed September 22, 2020. https://www.genome.gov/genetics-glossary/histone

CHAPTER 2

Borunda, Alejandra. "The Science Connecting Wildfires to Climate Change." *National Geographic*, September 17, 2020. https://www.nationalgeographic.com/science/2020/09/climate-change-increases-risk-fires-western-us/.

Landguth, Erin., Zachary Holden, Jonathan Graham, Benjamin Stark, Elham Bayat Mokhtari, Emily Kaleczyc, Stacey Anderson, Shawn Urbanski, Matt Jolly, Erin O. Semmens, Dyer A.

Warren, Alan Swanson, Emily Sonte, and Curtis Noonan. "The Delayed Effect of Wildfire Season Particulate Matter on Subsequent Influenza Season in a Mountain West Region of the USA." *Environment International* 139, (June 2020): 5-6. https://doi.org/10.1016/j.envint.2020.105668

Meyers, David G. and C. Nathan DeWall. *Exploring Psychology in Modules.* New York: Worth Publishers, 2019.

Miller, Carol. "The Hidden Consequences of Fire Suppression." *Park Science* 28, (Winter 2011-2012). https://www.fs.fed.us/rm/pubs_other/rmrs_2012_miller_c001.pdf

National Aeronautics and Space Administration. "Global Climate Change: Vital Signs of the Planet." Date Last Modified October 7, 2020. https://climate.nasa.gov/vital-signs/global-temperature/

Radeloff, Volker C., David P. Helmers, H. Anu Kramer, Miranda H. Mockrin, Patricia M. Alexandre, Avi Bar-Massada, Van Butsic, Todd J. Hawbaker, Sebastián Martinuzzi, Alexandra D. Syphard, and Susan I. Stewart. "Rapid Growth of the US Wildland-Urban Interface Raises Wildfire Risk." *Proceedings of the National Academy of Sciences 115, (March 2018). doi: 10.1073/pnas.1718850115*

CHAPTER 4

U.S. Department of Health and Human Services. "Biosafety in Microbiological and Biomedical Laboratories." Date Last Modified December, 2009. https://www.cdc.gov/labs/pdf/CDC-BiosafetyMicrobiologicalBiomedicalLaboratories-2009-P.PDF

World Health Organization. "Laboratory Biosafety Manual: Third Edition." Date last modified 2004. https://www.who.int/csr/resources/publications/biosafety/Biosafety7.pdf?ua=1

CHAPTER 5

Liesowska, Anna. "Exclusive: The First Pictures of Blood From a 10,000 Year Old Siberian Woolly Mammoth." *The Siberian Times,* May 29, 2013. http://siberiantimes.com/science/casestudy/news/exclusive-the-first-pictures-of-blood-from-a-10000-year-old-siberian-woolly-mammoth/

Mueller, Tom. "Ice baby." *National Geographic,* May, 2009. https://www.nationalgeographic.com/magazine/2009/05/mammoths/

Rummer, Jodie L. "How Woolly Mammoth Blood Cheated the Cold." *Journal of Experimental Biology* 213, no. 15 (August 2010). doi: 10.1242/jeb.036624

Wong, Katie. "Can a Mammoth Carcass Really Preserve Flowing Blood and Possibly Live Cells?" *Nature,* May 30, 2013. https://www.nature.com/news/can-a-mammoth-carcass-really-preserve-flowing-blood-and-possibly-live-cells-1.13103

World Health Organization. "Laboratory Biosafety Manual: Third Edition." Date Last Modified 2004. https://www.who.int/csr/resources/publications/biosafety/Biosafety7.pdf?ua=1

CHAPTER 6

Aryal, Sagar. "General Aseptic Techniques in Microbiology Laboratory." *Microbe Notes* (blog). February 14, 2019. https://

microbenotes.com/general-aseptic-techniques-in-microbiology-laboratory/

Bonnet, M., J.C. Lagier, D. Raoult, and S. Khelaifia. "Bacterial Culture Through Selective and Non-Selective Conditions: the Evolution of Culture Media in Clinical Microbiology." *New Microbes and New Infections* 34, (November 2019). doi: 10.1016/j.nmni.2019.100622

Brandes, Nadav, and Michal Linial. "Giant Viruses—Big Surprises." *Viruses* 11, no. 5 (April 2019). doi: 10.3390/v11050404

Levin, Petra Anne, and Esther R. Angert. "Small but Mighty: Cell Size and Bacteria." *Cold Spring Harbor Perspectives in Biology* 7, no. 7 (July 2015). doi: 10.1101/cshperspect.a019216

Minassian, Angela M., Robert newnham, Elizabeth Kalimeris, Philip Bejon, Bridget L Atkins, and Ian CJW Bowler. "Use of an Automated Blood Culture System (BD BACTEC™) for Diagnosis of Prosthetic Joint Infections: Easy and Fast." *BMC Infectious Diseases* 14, (May 2014). doi: 10.1186/1471-2334-14-233

Passerini, Rita., Maria Cristina Cassatella, Michela Salvatici, Fabio Bottari, Cristian Mauro, Davide Radice, and Maria Teresa Sandri. "Recovery and Time to Growth of Isolates in Blood Culture Bottles: Comparison of BD Bactec Plus Aerobic/F and BD Bactec Plus Anaerobic/F Bottles." *Scandinavian Journal of Infectious Diseases* 46, no. 4 (April 2014). https://doi.org/10.310 9/00365548.2013.876510

Sirucek, Stefan. "Ancient 'Giant Virus' Revived From Siberian Permafrost." *National Geographic,* March, 2014. https://www.

nationalgeographic.com/news/2014/3/140303-giant-virus-permafrost-siberia-pithovirus-pandoravirus-science/

Smith, Kenneth. "The Origin of MacConkey Agar." American Society for Microbiology, October 14, 2019. https://asm.org/Articles/2019/October/The-Origin-of-MacConkey-Agar

Steward, Karen. "Gram Positive vs Gram Negative." Technology Networks, August 21, 2019. https://www.technologynetworks.com/immunology/articles/gram-positive-vs-gram-negative-323007

Tankeshwar, Acharya. "Bacterial Culture Media: Classification, Types, and Uses." *Microbe Online* (blog), July 24, 2016. https://microbeonline.com/types-of-bacteriological-culture-medium/

Tankeshwar, Acharya. "Robertson's Cooked Meat (RCM) Medium: Principle, Composition, Procedure and Uses." *Microbe Online* (blog), November 29, 2016. https://microbeonline.com/robertsons-cooked-meat-medium-principle-composition-procedure-and-uses/

CHAPTER 7

Behjati, Sam and Patrick S. Tarpey. "What Is Next Generation Sequencing?" *Archives of Disease in Childhood. Education and Practice Edition 98,* no. 6 (December 2013) doi: 10.1136/archdischild-2013-304340

Dove, Alan. "Shotgunning the Messenger: Single-Cell RNA Sequencing." *Science,* February 21, 2019. https://www.sciencemag.org/features/2019/02/shotgunning-messenger-single-cell-rna-sequencing

Fox-Skelly, Jasmin. "There Are Diseases Hidden In Ice, and They Are Waking Up." *BBC,* May 4, 2017. http://www.bbc.com/earth/story/20170504-there-are-diseases-hidden-in-ice-and-they-are-waking-up

Heather, James., and Benjamin Chain. "The Sequence of Sequencers: The History of Sequencing DNA." *Genomics 107,* no. 1 (January 2016) doi: 10.1016/j.ygeno.2015.11.003

International Committee on Taxonomy of Viruses. "The International Code of Virus Classification and Nomenclature." Accessed October 10, 2020. https://talk.ictvonline.org/information/w/ictv-information/383/ictv-code

Peters, C.J. and Mark Olshaker. *Virus Hunter: Thirty Years of Battling Hot Viruses Around the World.* New York: Anchor Books, 1998.

Quammen, David. *Spillover: Animal Infections and the Next Human Pandemic.* New York: W. W. Norton & Company, 2012.

Schoales, Jeremy. "How Does Sanger Sequencing Work?" *ThermoFisher Scientific* (blog), June 17, 2015. https://www.thermofisher.com/blog/behindthebench/how-does-sanger-sequencing-work/

Schreiber, Melody. "The Next Pandemic Could Be Hiding in the Arctic Permafrost." *New Republic,* April 2, 2020. https://newre-

public.com/article/157129/next-pandemic-hiding-arctic-per-
mafrost

CHAPTER 8

Connolly-Andersen, Anne-Marie., Heather Whitaker, Jonas
Klingström, and Clas Ahlm. "Risk of Venous Thromboembolism Following Hemorrhagic Fever With Renal Syndrome:
A Self-Controlled Case Series Study." *Clinical Infectious Diseases* 66, no. 2 (January 2018). https://doi.org/10.1093/cid/cix777

Harrington, Samantha. "How Climate Change Affects Mental
Health." *Yale Climate Connections,* February 4, 2020. https://
yaleclimateconnections.org/2020/02/how-climate-change-af-
fects-mental-health/

CHAPTER 9

Binns, Corey. "New Insight Into How Blood Clots." *Live-
Science,* November 6, 2006. https://www.livescience.com/4300-
insight-blood-clots.html

Litvinov, Rustem I., and John W. Weisel. "What Is The Biological
and Clinical Relevance of Fibrin?" *Seminars in Thrombosis and
Hemostasis* 42, no. 4 (June 2016). doi: 10.1055/s-0036-1571342

National Institute of Biomedical Imaging and Bioengineering.
"Computed Tomography (CT)." Date Accessed October 11, 2020.
https://www.nibib.nih.gov/science-education/science-topics/
computed-tomography-ct

U.S. Food and Drug Administration. "Radiation-Emitting Products: Computed Tomography (CT)." Last Modified June 14, 2019. https://www.fda.gov/radiation-emitting-products/medical-x-ray-imaging/computed-tomography-ct

AUTHOR'S NOTE:

Johns Hopkins University of Medicine. "COVID-19 Dashboard by the Center for Systems Science and Engineering (CSSE) at Johns Hopkins University (JHU)." Date last updated October 11, 2020. https://coronavirus.jhu.edu/map.html

U.S. Department of Health and Human Services. *Justification of Estimates for Appropriation Committees.* Washington, DC, 2020. Accessed September 15, 2020. https://www.cdc.gov/budget/documents/fy2021/FY-2021-CDC-congressional-justification.pdf

www.ingramcontent.com/pod-product-compliance
Lightning Source LLC
Chambersburg PA
CBHW051448050726
47593CB00005B/1976